Married to a
ROCK STAR

Acknowledgments

Certainly, this book would not have been written had it not been for my husband's incredible, unstoppable, high-energy, audacious, and God-given talents in both the musical and political arenas. The support he receives on a daily basis from thousands of people across this country gives me proof that he is, and we are, on the right path. My love for him grows with every minute of every day as I watch and learn from the (whack) master.

I have been ultimately blessed with the birth of our son, Rocco, who has given my life true and indescribable meaning. I thank God every minute of every day for every breath he takes.

And obviously, I wouldn't be here if it weren't for my loving parents, Yvonne Messick and Ervin Strem. Their gentle guidance and compassionate directing of my childhood kept me from getting into trouble (and going to rock-n-roll concerts!). They always made certain that at least one parent attended my sporting events or school activities and kept me from eating bad food and making bad choices. My brother, Guy, desperately tried to introduce me to rock-n-roll as a teenager, but I simply wasn't buying it. I secretly wanted to keep up with my older brother and from that I learned competitiveness. (And although you can still beat me in swimming and motocross, Guy, I'll race ya in snow skiing!)

My stepchildren, Sasha, Toby, and Starr, and grandchildren, Riley and Jack, are all wonderful blessings of being in a blended family. I have been richly blessed by all of you, learned from you, and thankful that we share this journey of life together.

My wonderful friends and relatives who have shared in both the wildly crazy fun times and harrowing moments have provided me with more strength and comfort than I ever thought I could muster: Nancy Dobreff, Gram (Ruth Cowan), Misti Reidell, Stephanie Mayo, Anna Strem, Linda Scarpuzza, Marilyn Schneider, Valerie Guido, and Carla Nugent.

And although only my name is clearly written in bold as the author, so much goes into writing this book that it becomes a huge Nuge team effort. Ted was, of course, my main-squeeze editor. (It was difficult to get all of those Jacuzzi bathtub editing sessions accomplished, but we did it!) Thanks to my new kamikaze assistant, Linda Peterson, and faithful warrior butt-kicking bookkeeper and friend Kevin Ackley. And to editor-in-charge Jay Cassell, telephone buddy Laura Jorstad, Lisa Purcell, and to all of those at Lyons Press for believing in the Nugent Dream. Also a hearty handshake to the huge NugeTribe: Jim and Penny Lawson, Connie Strine, Paul Wilson, Traci Boyt, Ward and Krysten Parker, Calvin and Melissa Ross, and all of the many people who have supported Ted Nugent United Sportsmen of America, Ted Nugent Kamp for Kids, and Queen of the Forest throughout the years. God bless you all!

INTRODUCTION

Ted Nugent

WHAT IS A ROCK STAR, AFTER ALL? SHOULD WE BE IMPRESSED? I am more appreciative of a good welder or shotgunner than of the typical rockpunk. Certainly we have witnessed and celebrated truly astonishing musicians in our lifetime, music created by people who were brilliantly blessed by God with talents and artistic visions that captivate the soul of man. My life would be far less without the tribal rhythms so brilliantly crafted and delivered by Chuck Berry, Bo Diddley, James Brown, and so many others. Could we have ascended (or is that descended?) to such partying heights (depths?) without the outrage of defiance that the Rolling Stones and often the Beatles soundtracks provided? Could we have soared on the musical wings of an eagle without Jimi Hendrix? I doubt it, and I salute, congratulate, and applaud these virtuosos for their creative contributions to our quality of life.

That being said, what about their quality of life? What kind of pathetic brain-dead numbnut would follow in the footsteps of so many stoned clowns into their puking and dying orgy of stupidity? How many corpses does it take to indicate a pattern here? Too many obviously, and ergo the dynamic of the poor, pitiful rockstar who just can't stand those pesky brown M&Ms. Fuck 'em all.

I knew I was different, and though constant accusations of egotism flew (fly) like so many uncontrolled boogers at a Grateful Dead concert, I ignored the losers and continued on my TruNorth course to be the best that I could be. I ain't perfect, but I try like hell. Anybody who fails to believe and strive to be special has already lost the race. The American Dream is about optimizing your daily life and the gifts from God that provide it. I know many in the rock-n-roll industry who are hardworking, dedicated, extremely bright, and amazingly talented who also defy the presumed stereotype of the "rockstar." You can tell by the way they carry themselves. Usually. The entertainment industry and media overall are consumed with misrepresenting people whenever titillation can be magnified or even created out of thin blue air. So be it.

When you're smart enough to bust your ass with a gargantuan work ethic and clear sense of self to accomplish your dreams, you tend to avoid the lessers among us. Thankfully there are wonderful human beings all over the place to keep the campfire going, and I continue to hang with the best of the best, from my band mates Marco Mendoza and Tommy Clufetos, to my close-knit team of American Dream Commandos Linda Peterson, Doug Banker, Bobby Quandt, Jim and Penny Lawson, Ward Parker, and so many others, including rock stars of extreme merit like Sammy Hagar, Steve Tyler, Joe Perry, and many others whom I see year after year, some for more than thirty-seven years.

And quality people make quality of life. But *the* most important people of all are family. I love my brothers and sister and sons and daughters with all my heart and soul, but the most dynamic connection in life is the bond between husband and wife, for between these two people explodes every human experience possible in all the potential fire and ice man is capable of. I give you my soulmate wife, Mrs. Shemane Nugent.

I admit I did a lot of shopping around before discovering this beauty. I needed maximum mind, body, and soul with a spirit straight from the hand of God. She deserves me. Together we continue to ascend new heights high on heretofore undiscovered mountaintops and occasionally, as she most painfully shares in this book, the deepest, darkest pits of mankind's most insane, foolish, bad, and ugly. I put everything I've got into being a good guy, but like I said above, I ain't perfect. When I do good, sometimes it's truly something special to behold. And sadly, likewise, when I blow it, I really, really blow it big-time. My blowing it oughtta be done with now, and I can promise with supreme confidence that my heart and mind would never let me hurt those I so dearly love ever again.

I had and have my doubts whether this exposé is the right way to go, but for the therapeutic and educational offerings stated by Shemane, I am ready to let it rip with her. At the tender age of fifty-four, my career is an absolute riot. My life glows with dynamo sensations every day, in no small part due to Shemane's and my oneness. America is at war as it damn well must be, and emotions run high across the land. As I say in "Stranglehold," "Some people wanna get high, some people gotta start low. Some people think they gonna die someday, I got news ya never gotta go." We will leave our mark for the better, together.

Prelude

As I looked around me that exceptional afternoon in the summer of 2002, everything seemed to be perfect. The periwinkle sky was devoid of any clouds, and the air was fresh and free from the typical midwestern humidity. During a rare moment of solitude, I sat on top of a lounge chair next to our guitar-shaped pool and watched my son, Rocco, and some friends play basketball. In a sea-green field nearby, our horses nibbled hay and occasionally whipped their long tails to chase away the pesky flies. Birds sang and chirped their peaceful songs, as if to get my attention, perhaps to tell me that everything would be okay. Everything *seemed* to be perfect, but why did I feel as if there were a suffocating sensation tightening in my throat? Or like I could cry at the drop of a hat? No, make that at the mere sight of a hat. Despair and sorrow seemed to hang around me like weekend guests who stay for a month. For the second time in the fourteen years since I've been married to Ted, my weight had dropped below one hundred pounds. My health, I feared, was in grave danger. Just weeks ago, Ted had rushed me to the hospital with yet another debilitating migraine attack. Migraines torment me almost weekly now, but they only crept into my life slowly, painfully, after January 21, 1989, the day Ted and I were married. Before then I could have been the walking poster child for health and fitness, winning awards like "Detroit's Most Physical Female," and teaching a dozen or more high-impact, high-intensity aerobics classes per week. Now, when I don't have a migraine, I almost always have at least a torturous headache. My fortieth birthday was just a few days ago, but I feel well beyond those years. Deep dark circles etch my eyes and pimples dot my sallow skin as if I were a teenager. My once vibrantly healthy body feels as though it has faded into a painful array of maladies; as if I'm seventy years old.

Sometimes that's what being married to a rock star can be like.

Printed so neatly on the following pages are the tales of what my exciting, yet sometimes challenging life is like as Mrs. Ted Nugent. On the surface, rock stars' wives may appear to have it all. With red-carpet treatments at restaurants around the globe, first-class upgrades on airplanes, and courtside, ringside, or rinkside seats to nearly any sporting event imaginable, there are certainly perks to being the wife of a legendary musician. And there's no denying the fact that there's something incredibly sexy and tantalizing about sharing towels with a man who performs on stage in front of millions of people during his lifetime, tempting them with sweaty skin and hip thrusts that would make Elvis blush, but then again, there is a price to pay. In *Married to a Rock Star,* I will describe the price tag for all this grandeur.

Not for any of the aforementioned reasons, however, but because my husband and I share a deep love that cannot be measured, I am the luckiest woman alive. Ted and I took a brief excursion to hell and back and survived, and to this day remain best friends, lovers, and soul mates. We are truly one. Even after fourteen years of marriage, when my husband wraps his arms around me and kisses my neck before we fall asleep, I smile and thank God that I have him.

But Ted Nugent is no ordinary rock star, and my current elevated stress level is a direct result of the unrealistic approach he has of taking life "by the balls." While most people might have languidly eaten from the fruits of their labor, bought an island and relaxed, Ted continues to plant more apple trees and work harder than any ten or twenty men combined, stopping as infrequently as possible to taste the fruit he has worked so hard to cultivate and harvest. Unlike other recognized musicians whose careers may have started as quickly as they stopped, Ted's livelihood has defied gravity. Reaching success in the music industry at age seventeen when his "Journey to the Center of the Mind" hit the charts just as he was fresh out of high school, young Nuge had a ravenous appetite to play his guitar for as many people as he could. Today, with adult kids in their twenties and thirties and two grandchildren, Ted possesses precisely the same ambition for which he was always famous, but now his aspirations and interests have broadened somewhat to include environmental issues, wildlife management, political affairs, and, of course, Second Amendment rights.

Not that he hasn't always felt passionately about these subjects in the past, but with age comes a particular amount of maturity, wisdom, and refinement. He spends hours daily as a writer for more than thirty publications such as *Razor* magazine, the *Wall Street Journal,* and dozens of sporting and conservation publications. Almost single-handedly he writes, edits, and publishes *Ted Nugent Adventure Outdoors* magazine. Together we edit and produce an award-winning outdoor television show, *Ted Nugent Spirit of the Wild.* He is a third-term member of the board of directors for the National Rifle Association, not to mention numerous charitable organizations that he heads such as his own successful Kamp for Kids. And let's not forget to mention the obvious. He pours his heart and soul into hundreds of concerts every year, *still.* Although Ted vows to slow down, it seems that we continue to add more irons to our ever-burning bonfire.

It is because of Ted's current interest in politics that I've been fortunate enough to meet people like Charlton Heston, Vice President Dan Quayle, G. Gordon Liddy, Oliver North, Sean Hannity, Alan Colmes, Bill Maher, Michigan Governor John Engler, and more senators and representatives than I have room to discuss. You'll see many of their photographs in the "Nugent Family Album," on page 139. But wherever we go, law enforcement officers, judges, attorneys, and government officials take a moment to seek Ted out and thank him for standing up for the American public and their freedoms. Even before Ted came into my life, I shared more than just coffee with a few well-known celebrities, too. Radio talk-show host and author extraordinaire Mitch Albom was actually one of my co-workers when Ted walked into our radio station on October 4, 1988, the day we first met. Although Ted often says I lived a sheltered life before we met, there was one adventure I had with a famous actor—an actor who once gave Ted a co-starring role in his popular 1980s hit television series *Miami Vice.* (You'll have to read on to find out about Don.)

No, my life has not been dull. Imagine having Aerosmith's Steven Tyler running around your dining room playing laser tag with your son! Or being able to pop into a concert and hang out backstage with Joe Perry, Sammy Hagar, Kid Rock, Gene Simmons, Paul Stanley, Jon Bon Jovi, David Lee Roth, or Tommy Lee. In *Married to a Rock Star,* you'll get inside information about what it's really like backstage at a rock-n-roll concert. You'll read about meet-and-greets, riders, and groupies (unfortunately), and the lavish extravagances in which many superstars indulge. There are major trials and tribulations, too. In *Married to a Rock Star* you'll read about Ted's financial successes and debacles.

This, however, is not just a "tell-all" exposé. There is a method to my madness for toiling many months penning this book. Although Ted and I have had a few difficulties during our marriage, there has never been a time when I have been less in love with him than the day that we were married. It is primarily because of these marital tribulations that I have had to learn how to turn obstacles into opportunities. Our marriage, having been both blessed with infinite happiness and marred by formidable circumstances beyond my control, has actually blossomed during our fourteen years together. And that's no easy feat, especially in the entertainment industry where people change sex partners as often as their shoes. Perhaps sharing my story can lead someone out of their dark night and into the light of day.

One more thing you'll dig up when you read *Married to a Rock Star* is that somehow, in the midst of all the intensity, I became a Christian in a rock-n-roll world. *Go figure.* At a time when I was utterly confused about how I ended up married to a rock-n-roll musician who lived off the land like some kind of Grizzly Adams born a hundred years too late, when I wondered why I had to endure lengthy separations and groupies grappling at my husband's tail, I discovered an omnipotent force that curtailed my fears and led me down a path I never thought I'd take. For anyone who is enduring difficulties, I've weaved in my own personal messages about how to conquer obstacles and awaken our own divine potential. *That is why I have written this book.*

Married to a
ROCK STAR

Chapter One

Need You Bad

THE BRILLIANT SAPPHIRE SKY SEEMED BIGGER THAN EVER THAT September afternoon in Nashville. The intoxicating scents of summer lingered in the air along with a whiff of roasting hot dogs and fresh gunpowder. The rich country grass was as green as an emerald, and surely my eyes sparkled like diamonds as I watched my husband stop to chat with other musicians and movie stars at the Louise Mandrell Celebrity Shoot. Shotgun in hand as if it were just another appendage, Ted strolled toward me where I sat patiently, perched proudly on a nearby picnic table. He was ruggedly handsome with a casual jean shirt and pants gently accentuating his powerfully strong physique. His dark sunglasses heightened his classic and handsome face, and his long chestnut hair was pulled back into a ponytail. I saw all the things that had attracted me to him seven years before. Just sitting there, watching my husband from a distance, made my heart dance with exhilaration like we were newlyweds and not a seasoned married couple. Through our years together, I'd grown to love Ted more and more each day, and I knew that he felt the same. Nothing could possibly come between us. *Could it?*

Looking back now, however, I wonder if my memory serves me correctly. Wasn't it really cloudy that day? Didn't Ted look drawn and distressed? Maybe I was only seeing him the way I wanted to see him. The truth was, that day was going to be the end of a chapter in my life when I was naive, gullible, and too trusting. My world revolved around Ted, and I had lost control of who I was. My love for a man had never been so complete, nor so blind.

From the sapphire sky to the emerald grass to my twinkling diamond eyes, this was a time in which I saw the world through rose-colored glasses. Ted and I were perfectly in love with one another and nothing could change that. *Or so I thought.* What happened the next morning, however, transformed my life forever, and is the reason why I'm writing this book.

Typically, Ted had always been a crack shot. He couldn't miss. He could nail a clay pigeon with a shotgun blindfolded and one arm tied behind his back. Once, when he was conducting an interview during a pheasant hunt, he stopped to relieve himself. Fortunately, the cameraman respected Ted's privacy and turned the camera off, but he was sorry he did. This poor videographer missed an opportunity for the most outlandish video imaginable. Just yards away from Ted, a pair of pheasants flushed out of the brush and, with one hand busy and a shotgun in the other, Ted killed both birds dead center, one-handed, all while finishing his task.

Before Ted and I met, I had never held a gun in my hands. Now I shoot my Smith & Wesson Lady Smith handgun weekly, if not daily, practicing on our bowling pin and reactive steel plate shooting range, and I'm deadly! I've learned that a handgun is a necessary tool for self-defense. It's an equalizer, especially when there have been animal rights activists who, strangely enough, have threatened to kill our family because we choose to eat meat. So, yes, I'm armed and I'm dangerous. I have a lifetime date with my family, and I'm keeping it.

At the Louise Mandrell Celebrity Shoot, however, Ted missed more than he hit. His timing seemed to be off, or his heart just wasn't into the event. It was all to raise money for charity, so his accuracy wasn't that important, and I assumed, by his relaxed demeanor, that his performance didn't really matter to him, either. Part of the allure of charity events is the *it's-all-for-a-good-cause* attitude. His lack of concentration, I suspected, was due to the fact that he had just finished a grueling, maximum-velocity hundred-day tour that had taken its toll. On the road Ted had been having a severe bout of insomnia. He had always been a maniac workaholic, but he had taken on more interviews than usual and agreed to do more meet-and-greets, which often lasted until moments before he hit the stage.

Just So You Know: *A meet-and-greet is a social gathering that local radio stations organize along with an artist's management in order to help promote concerts. Huge artists like Madonna don't have to do them. She barely has to do any promotion to sell concert tickets at all. Many other recording artists, however—from Aerosmith to Lynyrd Skynyrd to Ted—conduct advance radio interviews and line up meet-and-greets to help promote their shows. People win tickets to meet-and-greets by doing some crazy things sometimes, or just being a particular caller-in to a radio show. They are given specific passes that are good only for the meet-and-greet before the show, where they usually wait their turn to have an autograph signed and say hello.*

After a full day of traveling from one gig to the next and conducting as many radio interviews as possible, my husband would often give up precious downtime just before concerts to attend meet-and-greets and official Ted Nugent United Sportsmen of America (TNUSA) meetings in cities throughout America. He would spend well over an hour in a seminar-type format discussing everything from politics to wildlife management or how he got the "Stranglehold" guitar sound, and then sign autographs for everyone. Hundreds of letters and e-mails pour in each week confessing gratitude to Ted for his dedicated stance and colossal presence in the media. Like a moving freight train, he was unstoppable. And who could blame him? Cards from mothers who had lost sons and daughters to drunk drivers were like coal in his engine. A lack of sleep combined with a busier schedule equaled outbursts toward those of us who were close to Ted, but I knew better, or at least I thought I did. When the body doesn't have adequate rest, it just doesn't function properly. Ted was simply overworked. We all needed to be patient. This weekend charity event on one fine-looking September afternoon was just what the doctor ordered. It had to be.

It wasn't often that we were without kids or some sort of entourage, so it was a treat to be alone, just my husband and I, for a few days. The change from a fast-paced, insanely chaotic few months was a welcome respite for me, as well. So as I quietly sat on the sidelines watching my husband like a thrilled and contented mother at her child's first piano performance, I counted my blessings a million times. Together Ted and I were the proud parents of a healthy, smart, and handsome young son. We had been through seven years of marriage—no small feat for anyone in the entertainment industry. At times it seemed as though I had been through surging powerful rapids, leaving me with barely enough strength to hang on to the raft. But in our case, Ted was the strong and powerful raft that never failed me. As long as I hung on, I thought, he would carry me through the treacherous river and past the jagged rocks. As long as I kept a firm grip, we could make it. And then there were more tranquil times like this one when I felt as though I was safe and protected in his embrace. We had stayed afloat through the most violent, ripping whitewater rapids imaginable. And at that moment I realized everything had come together for me. The payoff was grand. The lengthy separations and constant schedule of touring and recording were winding down now. There was a light at the end of the tunnel. Little did I realize that that light was a freight train heading directly for me.

We were scheduled to leave our deluxe Nashville hotel suite the next day, so we spent the morning in bed and relaxed. I couldn't have been more content. We ordered fresh strawberries, croissants, and coffee and snuggled in our plush white hotel robes. CNN was on the television and Ted flipped the channels several times, as usual, but then he turned the television off, paused, took a deep breath, and then turned it back on again. It seemed as though he was about to say something, but instead he became almost uncomfortably quiet. I didn't ask what was on his mind. As we lay side by side, he brushed the hair from my face and held me close. I was so happy. I thought about the day we first met and how far we had come over the years.

Hey Baby: How It All Began

In late summer 1988, as the world's leading technologists began to consider how to modify computers to allow for the coming millennium and the potential Y2K fears, or possibly the end of the world, I was offered a fabulous opportunity to become part of a morning show for WLLZ, a popular rock-n-roll radio station in Detroit. Although I was not overly familiar with rock-n-roll, this was a stepping-stone for me—the opportunity I had been waiting for—and I jumped at the chance to get into the broadcasting industry. Having just completed a degree in radio/TV/film from Wayne State University in Detroit, I was eager to immerse myself into an exciting new job. This job would also help me forget the fact that my former fiancé had called off our wedding. I was devastated. So immersing myself in work, I thought, would keep my mind preoccupied and away from the fact that I had been dumped. It did.

The morning show team consisted of two men, Jim "JJ" Johnson and George, a guy who pretended to be wrestler "Dick the Bruiser." They had the type of morning show that covered local and national news, entertained strippers on occasion, and featured sports with soon-to-be-famous author Mitch Albom *(Tuesdays with Morrie)*. Detroit Pistons basketball star John Salley showed up once or twice a week, and there was a female newscaster who seemed to be threatened by me, the perky new Traffic Girl. After a couple of months had gone by, the news reporter asked me why I smiled so much, and it wasn't until then that I realized that I had gotten past my failed attempt to walk down the aisle and that I was, indeed, happy. Besides relaying brief blurbs about traffic jams in the Motor City, I was really just there to banter with the morning crew and add a quick quip here and there. John Salley bantered with me a bit more than anyone else, off-air especially, but isn't that what basketball stars do?

My new job brought a much-needed change and excitement into my life. Musicians and politicians sauntered through our station hallways for interviews almost daily, slowly introducing me to the politics of rock-n-roll. For the first time in a long time I felt as though I was back on track, and I vowed not to fall off again.

Then Ted came into my life.

My boss, the radio station's program director, called me into his office and gave me a briefing on a forthcoming guest disc jockey named Ted Nugent, who would be filling in for the vacationing morning crew each morning for an entire week. "They call him the Motor City Madman. He's wild, too. He might ask you to do the traffic reports on his lap," my boss proclaimed.

"I can handle myself," I retorted, although I wasn't totally certain I could.

From the moment Ted strolled beneath the flashing ON AIR sign, into my workplace and life, a feeling of excitement and apprehension overtook me. Ted Nugent alarmed me. He was tall, larger than life almost, and he had powerful presence, something that went beyond his celebrity status. At first I was frightened of becoming intoxicated by his charisma. While men wanted to shake his hand, girls giggled and asked for his autograph, which was a green light for Ted to make a flirtatious comment and turn on the charm. It was easy to see why many women found him attractive. He was raw and rare. Only a few of the musicians who came to the station for interviews were actually able to function without a manager or entourage. Those days, rock stars had the same image as blond cheerleaders—cute, sexy, but not always known for their intelligence. Ted, on the other hand, was both handsome and smart—a rare combination in the rock-n-roll world—and clearly capable of calling his own shots without a manager or bodyguard looking over his shoulder.

Unlike the other women at the radio station who seemed to hang around the studio entrance when the ON AIR light was off, hoping to catch the eye of the renowned guitarist, I tried to avoid his magnetic draw. When it was time for my traffic reports, I tried to maintain my usual routine. I sat where I always did—no closer to Ted than I would the other disc jockeys. The way in which I was drawn to this man from the moment we first met, however, was staggering. Silently I wondered, *Does he feel the same way?* There was a bit of harmless teasing and my friends told me that Ted's voice changed when I entered the room—they could hear it on the air! I tried to deny it, but maybe they were right! Nevertheless, when I returned to my desk after my traffic reports were over, a strange feeling of warmth coursed throughout my body I could not explain, nor did I want to.

My life strategy clearly did not include someone like Ted Nugent. Finally, I thought I had come to a point in my life where I was in control. But with him there, I was feeling both exasperated and ecstatic. A bad sign, I knew. More than once I had fallen for the wrong man, and I was beginning to recognize the same signs with Ted all too well. It reminded me a bit of my brief tryst with the famous *Nash Bridges* actor Don Johnson. We had met at a Michigan offshore boat race and, I'll admit, he was one of the reasons I was able to get over my ex-fiancé quickly. He was tanned and handsome with a sort of ruggedness that I liked.

My friend Misti and I had both been winding up with the *love 'em and leave 'em* types of guys when all we really wanted were meaningful relationships—maybe, eventually, marriage. Misti knew some people who were involved in the offshore boat races and asked me if I wanted to make the two-hour trip with her to see them. We really needed to do something fun, something wild, and seeing cute guys race powerboats seemed like more fun than I had had in a long time. At that time, *Miami Vice* was one of the hottest shows on television, and I remember telling Misti that it would be great to catch a glimpse of Don Johnson. By the time we got there, however, it was too late. We'd missed the start of the race and there were only a few people still hanging around the seawalls. So Misti and I just sat there on an empty dock, adding one more entry to our list of reasons why we were depressed. It was one of those scorching-hot summer days where everyone was looking for a shady tree or air-conditioning. After a while two guys who looked as though they were part of a boat crew approached us. We chatted about trivial things, and eventually they invited us into their motor home for an iced tea and relief from the sweltering heat. Several other people came into and out of the motor home while Misti and I were sitting inside talking with all of them, never feeling threatened by anyone in any way. In fact, the door to the motor home was open the whole time we were there. An hour passed, and then the race was over and we heard people approaching. Our two new acquaintances got up, excused themselves momentarily, and then returned with an extra person. My body froze and a smile snuck out from the corners of my mouth as I saw Don Johnson enter the motor home. *We were in his motor home!* The guys we met actually worked for Don. Although I tried to maintain my composure, the *Miami Vice* actor was charming and boyishly affectionate, offering Misti and me another desperately needed cold drink. His magnetism was so powerful that I could barely speak when he sat down beside me and started making some fawning conversation. Misti continued wooing everyone else in the motor home with her beauty and grace while Don and I got to know each other better and talked about everything from the weather to the boat race. I don't even remember how he'd done, and it wouldn't have mattered to me if he'd lost anyway. Just being there with him was the grand prize.

My rendezvous with Mr. Miami came at an unexpected time—and although it helped me move past one relationship, it also proved that, at the time, I wasn't very good at selecting potential boyfriend material. So I vowed that no man would interrupt my progress toward becoming the next Diane Sawyer. And I reminded myself of that every moment I was with Ted.

When we were together at the radio station, it was an effort for me to concentrate on my work. He would always try to add a silly comment to my traffic report that would make me giggle like a schoolgirl, which the station management, I assume, thoroughly enjoyed. There was something about this man that intrigued me. He didn't give in to the stereotypical rock-star fashion ensemble: leather and chains. Ted was different. In fact, he possessed a rather atypical viewpoint on drugs and alcohol—*he didn't use them.* I, too, was an advocate of healthy living, teaching five to ten aerobics classes per week and overly concerned with every calorie I ate, as most people are. It amazed me that I had found someone who, like me, didn't indulge in either drugs or alcohol, but that I had to go to the rock-n-roll world to find him.

During our week together I had the opportunity to witness Ted in action, not on stage with a guitar, but with his lips snug up to a microphone for hours at a time discussing current events, politics, hunting, and, of course, a little bit of rock-n-roll. Those five days we worked together became a crash course in everything *Nuge* for me. Ted was captivating, interesting, and intelligent. He was nothing like I thought a musician would be, but then again, I hadn't given musicians much thought before I met Ted.

The Nugent name never entered my vocabulary until I witnessed the superstar in real action. Ted possessed the kind of rare and honest talent that I had never seen before, and one morning at the radio station, Mitch Albom, an accomplished pianist, brought in a keyboard and challenged Ted to jam with him. It was the first time I had ever seen Ted play. Watching his fingers move so quickly on the guitar neck had me mesmerized. The dynamic sounds made by just two men gave me a whole new appreciation for a type of music I hadn't previously considered. Although I realized it was machine-made music, I used to live to go out dancing to techno and disco music at nightclubs. That is, of course, until Ted came along.

As a midweek reward for great reviews, the radio station executives took all of us out to eat after the show on one cool October day. A distinct difference in Ted's behavior that day took me by surprise. He held the door for me and insisted that we sit next to each other, which, I feared, would only be a foolish move. Whenever our legs or shoulders brushed up against each other, my heart jolted and a dizzying current raced through my body. He told absurd jokes and I laughed uncontrollably. Our eyes met often and when they did, my body warmed as if I were drinking schnapps, on a cold winter day. I was falling fast, hard, and deep, but I wasn't about to let him know it.

When Ted leaned over and sampled food off my plate, I was shocked but, strangely, delighted too. *Was he flirting?* Yes, and it was the first time that his intentions were publicly aired. There was more to this outing, however. He was also allowing me to share in his love for food, and that felt comforting. It made me realize that there were no facades in Ted's life. He was very candid and opinionated, which was a contrast to the city guys who were primarily interested in discovering Victoria's Secret.

Although I've always been wary of gaining even two pounds, *I do love food!* I love different textures and tastes and experiencing tantalizing combinations of different cuisine. There's no denying that delectable food is sensuous and an incredible aphrodisiac. The first time we shared food was probably the first time Ted and I both understood we had advanced to the next level. Looking into each other's eyes as we sampled mouthwatering bites of scrumptious exotic food in harmony was certainly a healthy start to a steamy relationship.

But there was more than a friendly ease to the sexual tension between us, and we both knew it. Desperately, I tried to deny it, because I was scared to death to be hurt again. *He's a rock star, for goodness' sake.* Certainly Ted Nugent was not the marrying type. *Right?* But then he shocked me the next day when he called his mother while we were on the air. He said, "Mom"—while staring deep into my eyes from the other side of the soundboard—"I'm going to bring Shemane down to Florida to meet you. She's the one."

My heart stopped. I know it did. A stabbing pain cut my throat. I couldn't breathe. Adrenaline raced through my body, numbing it. I was bewildered and beguiled by this vibrantly authentic wildman, but I managed to hide my feelings, at least I thought I did. There were times that week when I wondered whether my fantasy had entered the reality stage. No, Ted's comments to his mother were just radio shtick. *Weren't they?*

Our physical attraction escalated each day as we eased into cushy chairs in the small confines of the broadcast station. The more I tried to reject the waves of voltage between us, the more powerfully I was affected. Although I spent most of my off-air moments in the shared office I had with Mitch, pretending to keep myself busy while Mitch typed and typed and typed, by the end of the week Ted was following me there like a lost puppy. On the last day, when Mitch had left the office for the studio to do his sports report, Ted came into the room, closed the door, knelt down on one knee, and asked me for a date. This man possessed a sense of excitement and power that I had never before experienced. From his black leather jacket to his long wavy hair, Ted epitomized the bad-boy image. I, on the other hand, was more like a Catholic schoolgirl. My idea of a short skirt was just above the knee. Together we were a dangerous recipe for an exciting brew. I knew it, he knew it, and everyone else in the studio was beginning to sense it, as well.

Although Ted had asked me out for a date several times immediately after we began working together—and my heart had said an emphatic *Yes!*—my intellect wanted nothing more than to walk away from this man and call it a day. After all, wouldn't I end up liking him and then being dumped again? It wasn't worth it, so I finally did what I felt I had to do and declined. "Catch of the Day" was not a title in which I was interested.

For more than a week after he left the station, however, Ted Nugent the hunter stalked his prey. Like a deer in the woods, I dodged his arrow as best I could. Somehow my boss must have heard about Ted's hunting maneuvers and was only too eager to do a little scouting for the Motor City Madman. His mind was most likely spinning with thoughts of promotion for the radio station, and meanwhile, I was worried about falling in love with a man and then getting dumped, wondering if it was all just a game to this rock star. Did he roll into each new city with thoughts of new, young conquests? Certainly I didn't want to be just a notch on the bedpost, and I reminded myself of that when my boss called me into his office. Our conversation went something like this:

"Mr. Nugent has requested your presence in Vegas."

"Oh yeah?" I said.

"Yeah, and I'd go if I were you. Don't worry about missing work. Hell, it'll be good for the station," he said with a grin that clearly resembled dollar signs.

After all, what other rock-n-roll radio station could boast a major celebrity dating one of its employees? Sure, it *would* be good promotion for the radio station. But I didn't want to even think about discussing my date with Ted on the air. I never enjoyed hearing about the sleazy strippers who sauntered into our station on occasion, and I didn't want any relationship I had to wind up being an opportunity to discuss romance and sex, especially if it could potentially ruin things.

Ted wasn't giving up either. "Because of my schedule, I don't have time to go on real dates," he pleaded to me during a telephone conversation. "I thought you might enjoy going to Las Vegas to see Sugar Ray Leonard and Donny Lalonde fight. Have you ever been to a fight before?"

"No," I said, trying to sound as if I couldn't have cared less about grown men fighting. In truth I was about to laugh and cry and scream at the same time. I couldn't believe this guy was asking me to go to Las Vegas!

"Come on, Shemane." It was his last attempt and I could tell he was about to give up. And then he said something that made me think about him entirely differently. "I'm bringing my kids."

With that, I presumed, I would be safe, safe from getting *too* involved, safe from the mesmerizing, almost brainwashing effect this forty-year-old man had on me. Ted assured me that his intentions were honorable, and I believed him. I rationalized that I could stay in a room with his fourteen-year-old daughter, Sasha, and Ted would stay with his twelve-year-old son, Toby. Maybe this could work.

On the flight to Las Vegas, Ted and I sat as close as possible to each other. As the minutes and hours passed, we touched more and more, both feeling and sensing a greater level of comfort and, of course, pleasure. We both read magazines, and caught each other's gaze. After a while, feeling uncomfortable and having the urge to stretch, I lifted my knee up and placed it over Ted's thigh. It just felt right, and it was, indeed, the moment our relationship changed. We were no longer working cohorts. There were no schedules to keep or telephones to answer. We were on a trip *together.* What happened during the next twenty-four hours changed my life.

When we arrived at the Las Vegas hotel and started to our rooms I began to feel uncomfortable. *What have I gotten myself into?* I had never been on an overnight trip with someone I was dating, and I suddenly felt like saying, *You know, I think I left my iron on. I'd better go home and check.* My inner voices battled while I contemplated my options, and then fate stepped in the way, setting me back on course. Our room keys didn't work!

Sasha and Toby went downstairs to play video games while Ted and I waited for a bellman in the hallway to bring new keys. For the first time since I'd embarked on this journey, I realized how irresponsible and intellectually vacant my decision to come to Las Vegas with Ted Nugent had been. As I slid down the wall and sat on the floor I asked myself, *What were you thinking?* Certainly I wasn't a prude, but spending the weekend with a man I'd only briefly dated was something I hadn't done before. Clearly, I was feeling unsettled about the arrangements and was even thinking that maybe I wanted *out!* Then, as if Ted could read my mind, I felt his gaze burn a hole right through me. Sliding down the wall and sitting next to me, he leaned over and kissed me so softly, like it was the first time for us both and he wanted to make sure he got it right. My breath quickened. My resistance subsided. Ted Nugent had me in a *Stranglehold.*

Caesar's Palace was filled with celebrities—Muhammad Ali, Joe Frazier, Howard Cosell, people who made more money in a day than I would in a lifetime. The bright lights and pandemonium were dazzling. My arm was wrapped around Ted's as we entered the arena. Cameras flashed and a crowd swooned to see the Motor City Madman. Ted introduced me to some of his rock-n-roll friends, Jon Bon Jovi and Richie Sambora, who were there and clearly excited to see the fight. Although I don't even remember who won, I had an indescribably wonderful evening. The night finally came to an end, and I still thought I might spend the night in Sasha's room. Ted said good night to his kids, closed their door, and gently directed me down the hall to "our" room. When we arrived, Ted took me in his arms and I melted. Absolutely melted. Waves of electricity shot through my body. The voltage was more intense than anything I had ever felt before. As our chests pressed against one another's, our hearts beat increasingly faster. His scent and his touch were intoxicating. He gathered me into his arms and I felt as though the world had disappeared. As he cradled my face with his hands I looked into his emerald eyes, and I thought I saw his soul. That was the night I fell in love with Ted with my body and my heart, and the moment I knew I would marry him. I knew the feeling was shared.

On the flight home my feet never hit the ground, even after the plane landed. It was difficult to suppress the elation I felt the next day at work. Concentrating on anything else but my new "boyfriend" was a steady challenge. I had to force myself to refocus. The co-worker who had always been especially irritated by my cheerful demeanor was even more annoyed when my behavior rose to new and happier levels for which Ted was responsible.

From that point on Ted called me daily and even drove a hundred miles one-way to meet me for a few hours. One weekend I reciprocated and drove the long, dark hundred-mile trip to his humble country home.

That night, in a dimly lit, rustic dining room, Ted played a song he had just written called "With My Friends." Unlike most of his fast-paced, high-intensity songs, this one was a deliciously syrupy ballad that seemed as if it was calling out to me. We came to know it as "our song," and he played it over and over again. Even with twelve-year-old Toby wrestling with his friends in the next room, it was difficult for us to get through the song without one of us becoming teary-eyed. I was in . . . *deep.*

Twenty-four hours a day, I thought about Ted but tried not to show my feelings. Once, when Ted was in New York writing songs with Tommy Shaw (the very beginning of the Damn Yankees), I cried because I missed him so much. Ted made my heart ache even worse when he suggested I call in sick for work and come to meet him in New York. The thought was enticing, and while in the midst of tears and trying to catch my breath, I did it! I called work and totally lost all composure. *Honestly,* I couldn't stop crying. The secretary just asked if I needed some time off, and I said yes. I never really had to lie.

With the stars shining brightly in a dark night sky, Ted proposed to me in a beautifully adorned suite at the St. Moritz Hotel in New York City. He played "our song" lightly on an acoustic guitar with the lights out. The people in the next room complained about the noise and the hotel manager asked Ted to put down his guitar for the night. We giggled and talked about having children and what our lives would be like for the next fifty years.

The next morning we shared a breakfast of wonderfully ripe strawberries with heavy cream, fresh-squeezed orange juice, and coffee. We couldn't have been more content if we were two birds in a birdbath on a hot day. My heart sang with joy as I glowed in the presence of my new husband-to-be.

One month later, at the radio station's Christmas party, Ted announced our official engagement. A month after that, just before his dear mother, Marion, passed away, Ted and I flew to Reno to attend a Safari Club International hunting convention. Several other celebrities were there, too, like Parker Stevenson and Kurt Russell; Ted and Kurt spent quite a bit of time together planning a celebrity hunt. Kurt's public relations assistant was there, too, bored and eager to do something, *anything*. Ted mentioned that we were planning on getting married that weekend. We simply wanted to go to a chapel, exchange vows, and become officially "hitched." The PR man, however, saw an opportunity to do what it is that public relations execs do best: plan big events in short periods of time. He encouraged us to let him help plan a wedding that weekend. In fact, he begged us to, and within forty-eight hours I walked down the most breathtaking aisle any bride could dream of.

My best friend, Nancy, flew in from Michigan during blizzardlike conditions to be my maid of honor, and together we found a dress in a little boutique in town and shortened it by cutting the lace hem with a pair of scissors. Kurt's magician got us the perfect flower arrangements, a fabulous cake, and, of course, press coverage—his specialty. Ted phoned his manager, Doug Banker, and asked him to fly into Reno for the festivities, as best man, but the first words out of Doug's mouth were spoken in his role as Ted's business manager: "What about a prenup?" Ted's answer was that he didn't need one, because, "Shemane's the one."

On January 21, 1989, Kurt Russell drove Ted around the famous Bally's stage in an antique motor car and dropped him off at the altar as I descended a staircase lined with (fully dressed) dancing girls. It was quite a production!

We exchanged vows in the early hours of the evening, in time for Ted to meet more people at his hunting convention, which should have been my first glimpse into the crazy, mixed-up world in which I was about to become involved. No one could convince me at that time, however, that I wouldn't always be the happiest girl on the face of the earth. Nothing short of a fortune-teller or some enlightened master telling me what my life would really be like as Mrs. Ted Nugent could possibly change my blissful, contented state. Maybe the master would say, *You will have a bright future, my dear. Yes. There will be much love between you and your husband, but also pain and suffering.* Would I have listened?

Only now do I wish that I'd met such a person. I wish there had been a way for me to have known the tremendous ways, both good and bad, in which my life would change. I wish I could have been forewarned. On the other hand, my rose-colored glasses were much too deep, dark, and thick for me to see anything but Ted. I was like a racehorse with blinders. Nothing would have kept me from marrying him. You can't always trust a fortune-teller anyway, now can you?

Chapter Two

Homebound

One hundred miles from my family and friends, I moved into the thick, mucky marshland of south-central Michigan, a zone commonly referred to as "Ted's World." Twenty miles from a decent-sized town, Ted and his children, Sasha and Toby, lived in a modest dark brown, wood-sided ranch home. There were dogs and cats, chickens and pheasants, and even a nasty old turkey that chased after anything that moved. This was not exactly where I thought a rock star might live, but since I knew little about the music industry, and didn't have any preconceptions, I wasn't tainted by the stereotypical rock-fan mentality. Destiny had brought me into the arms of a man who happened to entertain people. The fact that he lived humbly actually added credibility to my life-changing move. Ted was not the least bit swayed by any of the fashion or music industry's latest fads. Other than a satellite dish and a back room full of great-looking guitars, there was no sign that this three-hundred-acre rural homestead belonged to a man who had been North America's largest touring act in the late 1970s. No high-tech recording studio or sound system. In fact, I think he only had an eight-track stereo system and a portable cassette boom box that his kids mostly used.

The house itself was far from anything that could be featured on *Lifestyles of the Rich and Famous.* There were no dual ovens in the kitchen. In fact, there wasn't even a dishwasher. No luxurious pool or Jacuzzi. No sign of leftover party favors from rock-star soirees. A large black barn (that looked as if it was used in a Ralph Lauren ad) contained prehistoric farming equipment. Bales of hay lined the walls where a backhoe, several bicycles, and two motorcycles were sheltered. A battered brown pickup truck guarded the garage. Well-trafficked orange shag carpeting and paneled walls were prominent throughout the house, remnants from the 1970s. Majestic animal heads peppered the walls. Five or six adorned one room, ten the next. Bows, arrows, and guitars hung from the rafters in a cluttered family room that had buffalo and deerskins draped over couches and chairs, some auto racing trophies, gold and platinum albums, and, of course, deer antlers strewn everywhere. On the back cover of Ted's album *If You Can't Lick 'Em, Lick 'Em* is a photo of Ted nestled into a collection of guitars and other Nugent paraphernalia. Minus the guitars, that was how the living room looked when I first saw it. The closets were stuffed to the brim; most of my clothes had to be stored in the garage.

The house was so small that when Sasha and Toby grew too old to comfortably share a room, Ted created a bedroom for his daughter in the attic! There was no doubt that Ted Nugent was the most frugal man I had ever met.

Because of his hunting lifestyle, Ted literally lived off the land, farming hundreds of acres in corn and soybeans and harvesting the legal limit of deer each year. He provided his family with healthy, natural, and 100 percent legal sustenance that was chemical- and steroid-free. Living in the country was his escape from rock-n-roll's frenzied concrete jungle. It was definitely a way for Ted to keep himself and his children away from the morally depraved rock-n-roll industry and Hollywood. He could have lived anywhere, but he chose rural surroundings to plant his feet and his soul. Certainly raising normal kids in a promiscuous era is tough enough without having an environment muddled with excesses like alcohol or even drugs.

It is highly significant that Ted's kids have turned out to be responsible, considerate, and hardworking people when many celebrity children could be spoiled and lazy. One of Toby's first jobs (outside of being a roadie for dear old Dad) was a modeling assignment that had him on the pages of an Abercrombie & Fitch clothing catalog. He's now an attentive and loving dad himself! Sasha is an incredibly talented jewelry and handbag designer who manages our Ted Nugent Adventure Outdoors *magazine and our popular tednugent.com Web site. Starr is basking in the glory of raising her beautiful little girl, Riley. All three are terrific people with much talent and love to offer the world. I feel blessed to have them in my life and love them tremendously!*

There were times when I thought I would go crazy with boredom in this country setting. While I favored manicured lawns with perfectly placed flowers and sculpted hedges, I now found myself surrounded by the cornfields and cow pastures of Ted's World. There were times when I even questioned my swift decision to get married, quit my job, and reposition myself so far from my family and friends. But then there were moments when Ted would wrap his strong arms around me and make me feel as though everything would be all right.

For the first year of our marriage, Ted and I were together as much as humanly possible. When we needed milk, we went to the store together. We did chores together and went for wonderfully peaceful walks after dinner, hand in hand. My whole world revolved around Ted. That, however, would eventually wind up causing problems because I became dangerously dependent upon my husband, addicted to him, losing focus of the person I was inside. It was as if I had completely severed ties with my former life. My family visited for Thanksgiving, but other than that I rarely saw them or former friends. My love for Ted was almost reckless. It was as if I were standing on a beach before a tidal wave came, and I never even saw the storm coming.

I JUST WANT TO GO HUNTING

It wasn't long after our marriage that Ted delicately began to introduce me to the other love of his life. We spent our honeymoon on the famous Y.O. Ranch in Texas, and I renamed it the *huntingmoon*. Not exactly what I had in mind, but somehow, surrounded by exotic wildlife and thousands of acres of desolation, I didn't mind it. Besides, I knew that Ted would take me to Hawaii for the Kurt Russell Celebrity Hunt in a few months.

The Y.O. Ranch was equipped with real-life cowboys, like those I had only seen in movies. Talking with smooth southern drawls and wearing cowboy boots, Wrangler jeans, and Stetson hats, their courteousness and warm hospitality was a welcome change from the rude cabdrivers we encountered during our cross-country travels. Being with Ted was all that was important to me, so where we were didn't really matter.

The concept of hunting was alien to me at first. I was shocked when Ted was actually excited about waking up at four-thirty in the morning to get out into the woods and sit all morning in a treestand. He would even organize all his hunting gear—a bow and arrows, flashlight, camouflage clothing—the night before, like an anxious young boy the night before the first day of school.

There was so much more to hunting than I ever could have imagined. Although I knew that our ancestors from hundreds and thousands of years ago used bows and arrows and hunted for self-defense and to procure food for survival, I didn't quite understand why hunting was important to modern-day society. Like many who are unaware of the necessity for wildlife management, I didn't think about the fact that we, as a civilization, demand more and more shopping malls, highways, and homes, destroying millions of acres of wildlife habitat each year. Meanwhile, every year, almost every doe has at least one fawn—usually two. It didn't take long for me to understand that, although taking a living, breathing life wasn't something I wanted to do, I, in fact, was responsible for it, not just when I ordered a steak but also when I drove on a highway or even wore cotton clothing. Ted told me about how everyone, even animal rights activists, could not live on this planet without displacing millions of animals. Like so many people who are swayed by propaganda photos showing cute little raccoons caught in traps, I had never heard the truth told quite like this, but it all made sense. Hunting, I learned, wasn't at all like the image that the mostly liberal media and animal rights activists insisted this historical form of survival represented.

Some people also mistakenly believe that hunters just drive up to an animal and shoot it. For the vast majority of hunters, that's just not true. Just as there is a small group of Catholic priests who molest young boys, their behavior isn't remotely indicative of how the entire clergy operates. Hunting has gotten a bad rap from some of the media and animal rights activists. Many of them, however, cannot fathom the epic lengths to which outdoorsmen and -women go to safeguard clean air, soil, and water. Many people don't realize that it's the hunters, fishermen, and trappers who are the true conservationists, paying millions of dollars every year to safeguard precious wildlife habitat. Lots of people who mistakenly believe that hunters just want to kill every living thing would be surprised to hear the stories that I've heard from Ted over the years.

Night after night, day after day, Ted would come home with nothing but tales of breathtaking sunsets and dynamic sunrises bursting over the horizon and how he'd been entertained for hours by watching a squirrel, raccoon, or deer from a distance. You can talk about being outdoors and observing a magnificent sunset, but you cannot know what the experience is like until you actually take part in it, being fully present and taking in every ounce of dynamic color change. It wasn't that long ago, however, that our hunting heritage was not only welcomed but actually necessary.

My grandmother used to raise chickens, chop their heads off, and pluck them without flinching. Millions of people in much less civilized countries than the United States still survive and thrive that way on a daily basis. For most elderly people, it was a way of life. No one protested the fact that meat was on the table. It was food! Clearly the convenient, fast-food, fast-paced lifestyle many of us lead today must be overwhelming to someone like my grandmother. Words like *soy, tofu,* and *fat-free* were about as common as *e-mail, on-line,* and *html* in her day. They didn't exist. Neither did salmonella or *E. coli.*

A hundred years ago the concept of buying bottled water would have been absurd. Now we pay as much as two dollars in some airports for eight ounces of the clear liquid. A hundred years ago it would have been extraordinary for a woman to pay someone else to take care of her children while she worked. It would be even more unthinkable for an unmarried woman to get pregnant and raise her child alone.

We've come a long way, baby! Or have we?

We have morphed into a culture that our grandparents could not have predicted and probably don't appreciate. From pierced body parts to the Internet, we've moved mountains in just a few short decades. In many ways the advancement has been beneficial to our society—the information superhighway and better medicine, to name just two. In other areas, however, this liberal way of thinking has meant rejecting a lifestyle that actually served a purpose. Our hunting heritage brought wholesome food to the table, gave men a chance to exercise and bond, and provided an opportunity for the true cycle of life, the way God intended it to be fulfilled.

Ted was giving me not only a lesson in love, but also a lesson in life. Surely it would be difficult for someone like me who had rarely left the concrete jungle, to imagine having to kill my own dinner. Before I met Ted, I never thought I could harvest something on my own, but when he explained the way Mother Nature really worked and I had an opportunity to witness firsthand what hunting entailed, I could then make an informed judgment about it. Millions of families all over the world continue to enjoy living a hunting lifestyle in which they eat only what they kill, and basically live off the land. Many, I suppose, simply couldn't do it in this twenty-first century. Imagine having to chop your own wood to heat your home throughout the winter. We are one of the few but growing number of American families who are returning to this independent, self-sufficient lifestyle. Except for an occasional chicken, turkey, or lamb on holidays, we don't buy meat from the grocer. Our freezer is stuffed with venison and other wild game, and we eat what we harvest. When the tragic events of September 11, 2001, occurred, our telephone rang off the hook with family and friends calling to ask us if they could come to our house if the United States actually went to war. They knew we had everything necessary for complete survival for years.

When people give me that crooked-face look as soon as I tell them that we live off the land and mostly eat wild game, I explain my number one reason for doing so: health. Recent, unprecedented outbreaks of *E. coli* and mad-cow disease and reports from our own Centers for Disease Control that commercial, domestic poultry has *some degree* of salmonella poisoning are substantial incentive to consider steroid-free, chemical-free, all-natural wild game. Just as human beings are healthier when they get more exercise, so are animals that can run free, graze on natural grasses and forbs like clover, and eat apples fresh from the tree, or corn right off the stalk. The University of Colorado concluded in a study that eating wild game helps to reduce clogged arteries. *Pass the elk steaks, please.*

For those people who believe that abstaining from animal flesh is the way to go, I say, good for you. Vegetarians risk deficiencies in many important vitamins and nutrients such as calcium, iron, zinc, and riboflavin, but that's their choice. America is the land of the free, and they can make their own decisions about what to feed themselves and their children.

Since we've been married, I've only hunted a few dozen times; Ted hunts enough for both of us, and our freezers are always stuffed. I was resistant in the beginning of our relationship, but then, almost as if there was some kind of magnetic draw coming from the woods, I had to go back again and again. Sometimes I'd just get into a treestand with my video camera and wait for Mother Nature's exhibition. But every time I venture into the wild, I experience dynamic, almost spiritual awakenings. Sitting quietly in the woods, watching leaves gently spiral to the forest floor, I feel a peace and calm I've never known. The fresh air always seems to cleanse my entire body, mind, and soul to the degree that I truly feel one with nature, and experience a powerful spiritual connection with God. My body melts into such a relaxed state that I have to force myself to remain awake. It's meditation in its finest form. In fact, because I've been suffering from migraines, several doctors have reinforced my decision to venture into the woods, relax, and meditate. And when I do, there's no question that I feel healthier and more at peace.

Although Ted and many others can disagree with me all they want to, if they want to, I prefer to call hunting an *outdoor adventure,* because that's exactly what it is.

At first, encounters with wildlife are infrequent. In the woods, you are the intruder, you are penetrating wildlife habitat. Deer, squirrels, raccoons, and birds know every branch, twig, and blade of grass, so every move you make is noticeable to them. If you throw a stone in the water, waves ripple outward; similarly, animals are wary of your presence, and if one is startled and runs off, so will all the others. When you do finally see an animal, whether it's a rabbit, squirrel, turkey, or deer, your heart starts beating as if Billy Blanks is coaching you through your own private TaeBo session. It's exhilarating!

It's painstaking, too! Harvesting an animal takes years of patience and practice. Don't be fooled into thinking that anyone can pull out a gun or a bow and bring home the bacon. It took Ted fourteen years to harvest his first deer—more perseverance than most of us have. Since I had a great instructor, it took me less than a year for me to provide my family with sustenance.

When Ted first introduced me to this hunting, I never thought I could actually kill an animal myself. To this day, I still have qualms about personally being responsible for the death of a living thing, but Ted has enlightened me to the truth and I know that we, as hunters, are ultimately being more honest about the origin of our meals. The fact that so many people, myself included, continue to buy leather goods and products made from animals and build more houses and buildings—decimating thousands of acres of animal habitat each year, killing millions of pheasants, squirrels, raccoons, and so many other living creatures—confirms the fact that we must manage this precious resource. It was Ted who helped me realize that we cannot live on this earth without displacing millions of deer, songbirds, and game large and small. As we continue to encroach upon these precious creatures acre by acre, shoving them out of their homes so that we have the convenience of bigger shopping malls, better football stadiums, more golf courses, condominiums, and highways, they have less and less room in which to live. Consequently, there are hundreds of thousands of car–deer accidents each year, causing human fatalities and untold millions of dollars in property destruction and insurance fees. It's not unusual to see ten new road-killed animals *every day* in the country where we live, and that's with Michigan hunters harvesting 600,000 deer each year. What would happen without hunting seasons? It's not hunters who kill off a species and threaten its existence, it's the human race as a whole. Human encroachment is most often the cause of habitat destruction, while hunters' dollars pay for the maintenance and safeguarding of millions of acres of forests, swampland, and wild ground. Animal rights activists waste millions of dollars paying people to pass out misinformation, or send out death threats to people like us who choose to eat meat and serve their children milk when they have cookies, instead of actually doing something to protect what it is they so vehemently wish to preserve. Hunters are the real animal rights proponents.

A whole new way of thinking and looking at the world was introduced to me in the swampland of Michigan. For the first time I heard about the spirituality of hunting and what really compelled my husband to don a camouflage suit and wade sometimes waist-deep in a mucky marsh just for the opportunity to be outdoors. I learned about the connection Ted had with Mother Nature and how each time he watched the sun rise and set he gained a sense of peace and a greater awareness about his purpose in life. This wasn't the type of talk I thought I would hear from an alpha-male hunter like Ted, but I vowed to keep an open mind about these events as they unfolded, even the gutting process. Our trip to Idaho, however, was my first experience of what the Call of the Wild sounded and felt like. And it wasn't precisely what I'd anticipated.

Call of the Wild

I quickly learned that there were many facets to Ted Nugent's life, and if I was going to be any part of it, I'd better try to fit in somewhere. At times, however, I felt as though I was running alongside a freight train trying to jump on. I wasn't sure if I could ever keep up with Ted's frantic pace. He adapts to drastically different settings swiftly, like Clark Kent changing into Superman in a nanosecond. For hours upon hours Ted can be Mr. Gregarious and sign autographs for hundreds or maybe even thousands of people at a convention, taking pictures with babies like a politician, then easily transition into calmly, quietly stalking through heavy sawgrass as the sun descends. There's some heavy Zen going on there. He knows it.

Since I was used to working hard, and multi-tasking constantly, it didn't take me long to acquire the same lightning pace, and I learned to adapt to a multitude of dynamics in Ted's life. There was certainly never a dull moment early in our marriage. Shortly after our "huntingmoon," Ted and I started planning for the Kurt Russell Celebrity Hunt in Hawaii. There was, however, one small stipulation. Since I had enjoyed our "huntingmoon" so much, Ted reasoned, maybe he could take a quick side trip to Idaho on our way to Hawaii for a pronghorn antelope hunt. *Just a quickie.*

Although he warned me that we would be sleeping in a tent and hiking mountains during the day, the former tomboy in me got enthusiastic about a wild adventure with my new husband. It would be warm, romantic, and snuggly, I was certain.

Bound and Gagged

Our guide's battered Suburban bounced and banged its old frame over the heavy potholes and skinny trail that wound treacherously around the steep mountain. It took hours for us to get to where we were going—and that wasn't even to camp! We arrived at a holding spot of sorts where our guide transferred our luggage—packed not only for our Hawaii trip but also for this Idaho adventure—onto the backs of horses, and we finished the journey to camp on a painstakingly slow, eight-hour horseback ride. It took me a while to switch gears and completely leave behind the chaos of our home, with its six telephone lines, fax machines, and business obligations, but I soon began to appreciate everything from the crisp air to the warmth of the horse between my legs. For the first time I realized where the phrase *purple mountains majesty* came from, and I felt thankful that Ted had brought me. It seemed as though everything popped out at me like never before. When was the last time I had noticed the bright green color of trees so much? Or when had I ever gazed so contentedly at the hazy cerulean sky? When did I have the time? Maybe, I thought, hunting was just an excuse to spend more time outdoors and reconnect with every living thing.

My legs reminded me that I had not been on a horse in years, and it had been even longer since I had camped. As a child, my family had bivouacked only once or twice before, so I was a bit leery. Sure, I rode and raced dirt bikes with my older brother, Guy, and his friends, but I always went home to a hot shower and a warm bed. Before I met Ted, my idea of roughing it was going to a hotel that had no room service. Still, I wasn't too concerned about the accommodations on this trip because I knew Ted and I would be together. What else mattered?

When we finally arrived at camp, I was surprised to find that the bathroom consisted merely of a ripped-up lounge chair with an old toilet seat cover on top of it, blocked by a couple of bushes for privacy. Sitting on this new "toilet" wouldn't be the only challenge I was about to face. Things were about to get much worse.

That night, I truly thought I would die. Never before had I slept outdoors in freezing conditions with only a thin tent to block the wind. Although I had on every piece of clothing I'd brought, I remember feeling for the first time that I had gotten myself mixed up in a terrible mess. Surely there was no way I could survive sleeping in a tent when it was twenty degrees outside. Ted only smiled and held me close, assuring me that our body heat would be all that was necessary for us to stay warm. Obviously, he didn't know that I needed a sweater in any temperatures under seventy degrees.

Obviously, Ted was right. I survived. In fact, I was elated to discover that during the day, the Idaho fall temperatures soared into the eighties. A magnificent new world unfolded before my eyes while Ted and I spent a few days hiking the mountains, scouting antelope, and snuggling during the cold evenings. Hunting wasn't all that bad!

Ted and I departed our Idaho camp late one night after dinner in a borrowed car. We sat next to each other like the newlyweds we were and drove along the deserted highway, headed toward a hotel near the Boise airport. After the hundred-mile drive, we would catch a few hours of sleep and fly out of Boise for the Kurt Russell Hawaii hunt early the next morning. As I looked out at the desolate landscape, I silently wondered what we'd do if our car broke down. This was 1989, before the age of cell phones, and there were no houses, buildings, or even streetlights. We were alone with the stars and the tumbleweeds and, of course, each other. Curiosity, however, gnawed at me l and just as I asked Ted what we would do if our vehicle conked out, I looked at the speedometer and watched it descend.

"Are you going slower for a reason?" I asked as I gave Ted a concerned look. My husband has never been known for slow driving.

"No, I'm not," he said, and I watched helplessly as our car slowed from one hundred miles an hour to eighty, to sixty, to twenty, and finally to a stop. "I think I blew it up," Ted said as he drove the car off the road onto the shoulder and put it into park.

"Now what?" I asked, thinking it was quite a coincidence that I'd mentioned car problems as we were having them.

"We passed a bar about a mile ago. Maybe we can walk back there and call someone from the hunting ranch," Ted suggested.

Well, I was coming to the understanding that my life with Ted Nugent would never be dull. Just then, a car pulled up on the opposite side of the road and a young, strong-looking man got out. It turned out that the guy had left a tour of duty in the Navy and was on his way home . . . and just happened to be a huge fan of Ted's. He was more than happy to turn around and drive us to a phone, but we still had to contend with the broken-down rental car. In the end Ted's hunting buddy Mike Taylor made the trip during the middle of the night to rescue us and drive us to Boise.

Getting to Kurt's hunt in the tropical paradise of Kona, Hawaii, was a welcome relief, but one that wouldn't last for long. In order to give the hunters a more authentic experience, Kurt's public relations man came up with a plan that sounded good and looked great, but logistically was pure hell. Someone had gone to great pains to build individual thatched-roof huts along the beach for each group. Our hut happened to be about a quarter mile down the beach. The ocean glistened like diamonds, palm trees hung over the white sandy strand like a canopy, and grand volcanoes stood majestically in the background. I couldn't imagine anything more beautiful. Then we realized that the only way for us to get all of our luggage, hunting gear, and video equipment to our tiki hut was to carry it ourselves. We had all our bags and equipment from the Idaho hunt, including a twenty-pound camera and fifty pounds of equipment. We trekked on anyway. But when we arrived at our "home" for the next four days, we were slightly shocked to discover that there were only five-foot-long cots on which to sleep and a twenty-gallon jug perched upside down on top of the corner of the roof for a makeshift shower. When all I really wanted was a hot bath, it looked like I'd be getting another chance to fully experience the outdoors.

Ted and I, and most of the invited guests at the Kurt Russell Celebrity Hunt, ended up at a hotel that year. Goldie Hawn and the kids were there, swimming in the ocean and appearing to have a blast. At night Ted and country music legend Larry Gatlin played guitars and led everyone in songs by the campfire on the beach. Baseball great Billy Martin was there, too, just before he died, singing "I Just Want to Go Hunting" right alongside Ted, which I captured on videotape. Billy especially liked Ted's brand-new song "Kiss My Ass," and wanted Ted to sing it again and again.

MYSTIFIED

Ted and I were inseparable whenever he wasn't touring. My heart would always sink, though, whenever it was time for him to go on the road. Without him, I felt alone and lost. I was in the middle of nowhere taking care of the family, businesses, and the farm, none of which I minded at all. What I *did* mind was doing it all without my husband and being so far from my family and friends in the swamp hellzone of southern Michigan.

In just a short period of time Ted had become my whole life, my world, and I didn't even realize that I had become completely swept up by him, consumed as if by quicksand. There was no longer anything else of importance in my life. No job. No friends. Nothing. And when he left me alone to go on the road, I felt cheated and abandoned. Before we were married, I'd failed to consider the logistics of our relationship. I didn't realize that when Ted would be going on tour I was supposed to stay at home much of the time. I had always thought that we would never spend a moment apart.

Certainly, it was my fault for not clarifying what the schedule would be when Ted toured or even traveled. I simply hadn't stopped to think about what my life would realistically be like as Mrs. Ted Nugent. We rushed into an engagement and rushed into getting married. We were hopelessly, helplessly in total unabashed love and no one could have convinced us otherwise.

It was a bit of a wake-up call for me, when I moved into Ted's farm, however. In a matter of days he had me feeding a mean-ass wild turkey, shoveling dog crap, carpooling kids, and learning how to shoot a gun. Eva Gabor had nothing on me. It would be impossible for us, I knew, to ever live in a large city like New York or Los Angeles, because Ted needed at least a few hundred acres to roam. He'd much rather hop on an ATV or a horse and cruise through swamps than don an Armani suit and take me out to a lavish dinner. I realized that I'd have to be the one to compromise. While Ted lived in heaven, I just wished I could live in a town that had more than a gas station and a bank.

Ted wouldn't have it any other way and continued to try to convince me that this country lifestyle really *rocked*. The fresh air was intoxicating, I'll admit. And because we traveled so much, the isolation was, indeed, serene. Also, I do believe that a little bit of manual labor each day—chopping wood, feeding animals—builds character. It teaches children responsibility, and I've always loved animals, so taking care of the dogs and the horses wasn't a problem and was actually therapeutic for me. Eventually, I became more and more at ease with living in rural America.

Amid hundreds of acres of marshland and thick forests, it would seem as though there was little stress. Looks, I discovered, can be deceiving. We desperately tried to eliminate unnecessary appointments in our schedules, but everything seemed to be important, like spur-of-the-moment interviews on Fox News and CNN, and Ted and I found ourselves busier than ever. Swampland or not, when you have six telephone lines in your home, it can get pretty chaotic.

Although I didn't have a full-time occupation anymore, I found myself working exasperatingly long hours overseeing the bookkeeping responsibilities for the half dozen businesses that Ted and I headed together. It was a bit of a stretch from being a broadcasting reporter, but because of Ted's history with swindling managers, accountants, and attorneys (read more about this in Chapter 3), he needed me to play a big role in overseeing our finances. With his hectic schedule of rehearsing, recording, writing, and touring, it made sense for me to be the one to dive headfirst into that mystical maze of numbers and attempt to keep our accounts in order. It said a lot about our relationship that he trusted me 100 percent to manage our finances, and for that I was grateful.

Needless to say, shouldering the weight of such a responsibility was stressful. It did, however, keep me busy and oblivious to the fact that I was completely isolated in Ted's World. There were times when I regretted putting my career on hold to raise a family, spend time traveling with my husband, and manage our investments. My goal in life had always been to eventually replace Barbara Walters, but obviously that didn't happen.

If he fails to obey, do chores, or eat every last scrap of food on his plate, this child gets reprimanded big-time. Ted is the disciplinarian in our family. I'm the negotiator.

There's something about burping and farting and the male species that I'll never quite figure out, but Ted and Rocco seem to be in hog heaven when they discuss how big or how long they can let one rip. Frankly, I have better things to do, but I'm happy that they can find humor in the little things. It is funny to see and hear someone like Ted, the Motor City Madman, burp and fart on command to accentuate a point, or even hit a crescendo in a song. It's astounding, but most morning-show disc jockeys have had the opportunity to see him in action. Rocco, I fear, is picking up on this habit.

When Ted is home we're usually joined at the hip most of the day. We work in our home office together. He'll do telephone interviews and I'll edit the television show, try to squeeze in a quick workout on a Spinning bike or teach a kick-boxing class, and of course follow up with some yoga. Ted gets his exercise from baling hay and doing chores, but it just puts me in a better place physically and emotionally when I can spend a good quality hour solely on some substantial sweat exercise at least three times a week.

We take care of our animals together and go for walks in the woods, or go for horseback rides. We usually spend several hours in the office, and then take mini breaks throughout the day until it's time to pick up our son from school. On the average, Ted gives dozens of interviews each week to radio stations, newspapers, magazines, and television shows all over the world. While Rocco could be playing laser tag in one room, Ted could be on CNN or Fox in the next. He writes for more than thirty publications each month, in addition to spending hours each day communicating with thousands of rock-n-roll fans and TNUSA members on the tednugent.com web site. Not a day goes by when Ted's fingertips aren't at some point glued to the keys pouncing and poking. I've often wondered what he ever did with all the time he had before Al Gore so thoughtfully invented the Internet.

If he's not on his computer, Ted might also be found straddling a four-wheeler roaming the hundreds of wild forest acres that surround our lakefront home, looking for "spirit signs"—shed antlers or buck rubs. Most of the time, when Rocco isn't playing basketball with his friends, the three of us, and any neighborhood kids who happen to be around, go along for trail rides, discovering new or widely used deer trails, or just having a blast being outdoors.

Ted is intensely connected to the spirituality of wildlife and spends hours each day monitoring their behavior. We spend tens of thousands of dollars each year maintaining optimum quality of life for the critters that roam our property. We plant corn, soybeans, and alfalfa on hundreds of acres of habitat so that the deer have a source of protein during the long Midwest winters. As a result, we see dozens of whitetails, raccoons, pheasants, geese, ducks, squirrels, and other wildlife on our property every day. One of the biggest fallacies about Ted is that he wants to kill everything that moves. In reality, he is probably more of a wildlife conservationist than most animal rights activists, who often fail to practice what they preach. We donate thousands of dollars to wildlife restoration charities such as Ducks Unlimited, Delta Waterfowl, Rocky Mountain Elk Foundation, National Wild Turkey Federation, and dozens of habitat-specific charities that ultimately enhance overall biodiversity.

When he's not touring or giving interviews, the Motor City Madman is a Motor City MadDad! He is an affectionate and attentive father, calling Sasha, Toby, and Starr almost daily and sending them cards and flowers often. When he's home and not on a rock-n-roll or hunting tour, Ted attends nearly all of Rocco's basketball or hockey games (although he has been known to bring along his laptop computer once or twice). Hugs and kisses are endless at our house.

I do, but that's just the way I am. It always seems that on the rare occasion when I don't make our bed, that's the day a camera crew or MTV Cribs arrives unannounced.

Ted took Sebastian on our Sunrize Acres hunting grounds. Mother Nature was in all her glory as she showered the two rockers and camera crew with an abundance of thick white snowflakes throughout the day. The VH1 crew and Sebastian gathered at our house after the shoot to film us all delving into flesh from their harvest. Fortunately for VH1, we sent our camera operator (and commando caretaker) Jim Lawson to videotape the day's events. Just before we sat down to eat, I heard grumbling from the VH1 producer. In the midst of the chaos and snowstorm, the crew actually lost the videotape of an entire day with Ted and Sebastian. They spent hours searching for it, but obviously they never found it in the deep snow. Fortunately, our cameraman had backup!

As usual, Rocco was entertaining a few friends, and I do mean entertaining. This young lad derives great pleasure in amusing people and never misses an opportunity to add a quick comical statement or some sort of hilarious antic. He lives to make people laugh. At times Ted and Rocco vie for attention. While Dad is entertaining the VH1 crew, our son is meanwhile caught up in his own world of comedy and laughs. Eventually, of course, Ted's thunderous shouting and laughing tends to overwhelm the boys and everyone rushes to see how Rocco's dad has the entire VH1 crew and Sebastian Bach laughing hysterically from another insane joke.

Chapter Three

Stranglehold—The Business of a Rock Star

Managing a recording artist isn't always easy. Occasionally, as in the case of famous rock-n-roll celebrity superstar Ozzy Osbourne, family members are impressively involved in their spouse's careers. Ozzy's wife, Sharon, is his manager. While most rock wives don't get that involved, many of us know a lot more than we ever wanted, or thought we would. Some just stay home. A Rock-and-Roll Hall of Famer's wife (whom I know would rather not be mentioned by name) told me that she and her kids tour with her husband most of the time. They bring a tutor along for the kids and they relish the fact that they do not have a normal lifestyle and can afford to spend quality time traveling the world together. Meanwhile, other rock wives or long-term girlfriends just don't visit their spouses when the band is on tour. Their presence gets in the way of making music. It is difficult, especially when you have young children, but this particular Hall of Fame rock wife told me one thing I won't forget: "If I'm not there, someone else might be." She could be right. In any event, they're smart to stay together as much as possible as a family unit. Sometimes we have to reevaluate our situations and come up with a plan that will work for each one of us, individually. What works for our family might not work for others.

Every man is fallible and it's primarily because of that, I suppose, that rock-n-roll wives initially begin to travel with their husbands on concert tours. There's too much room for groupie interference, and we realize that if we're there, nothing can happen. Still, we just can't travel all the time; children need and crave normal routines and playtimes with friends. They need to see more than hotel rooms, concert venues, and airports. Being homebound, however, is very difficult on a marriage. Trust is threatened. The stakes are high. Initially, I remember, I wanted to go on tour because I couldn't stand to be away from my husband, but, yes, I'll admit, I wanted to check up on Ted and see what truly went on at a rock-n-roll show. When Ted began to complain about the sound, or lights, or something with the accounting and I was tagging along with nothing to do but read a trashy novel, he asked me to take on small tasks, like writing checks. Since then, my duties have grown considerably. Now, fourteen years later, I pay most of the tour bills and stay in daily communication with the accountant, banker, Ted's road manager, and his manager. Although these tasks are more than what I initially agreed to assume, I am happy that we can manage this production together.

Ted kept touring more, agreeing to do more speaking engagements, and more paperwork kept piling up on my desk. It wasn't that I didn't like to work, I just didn't enjoy working seventy hours per week. Anyone who has worked with Ted, however, knows that wearing numerous hats is par for the course. All of a sudden, it seemed, we had way too many businesses, way too many responsibilities, way too many potential crises.

The chaos and pandemonium in my life soon escalated to new heights. Emotionally and psychologically, I was exhausted and wouldn't have been surprised if I'd collapsed, even though I've always enjoyed almost perfect health. But by our fourteenth year of marriage I started to notice that my heart was racing repeatedly when I was just carrying on with daily activities like making dinner or doing laundry. I was constantly anxious about everything. It also seemed like much of what I did was somehow not done the way Ted wanted it to be done.

I wasn't walking on but rather running, jumping, and dancing on hugely jagged, broken pieces of glass.

Ted did what most successful people would do when things were spiraling out of control: He was occasionally harsh and critical toward those of us who were closest to him. Anyone who has worked for Ted knows that he expects and demands excellence in everything, but in Ted's World, you guessed it, an overabundance of things often seem to go wrong. As you can imagine, this makes the Motor City Madman one mad man. Ted can be overly demanding and even unnecessarily berating, but this behavior has its purpose.

After a recent concert in Texas, I could tell by the exasperated look on Ted's face as soon as I entered the dressing room that something was amiss. He didn't greet me with the typical I've-missed-you for-the-past-two-hours tight embrace and kiss that I usually receive after every show. I didn't have to ask, because I had seen several things go terribly wrong that night and the crew members were running around with very stern and disconcerting looks. "Do you feel okay?" I inquired, concerned with Ted's health.

He said nothing but shook his head and grimaced in despair. It was bad. There was nothing more for me or anyone else to say. Someone or several people had let him down, and he was far beyond disappointed. At least when Ted yelled, you knew what the problem was, but in this case the silence was so deadly that no one wanted to be anywhere near him.

We deal with almost entirely new lighting crews in each city Ted tours. Although our main lighting director stays on tour with us, it's his job to instruct the local crew members about lighting placement as he stands halfway back in the crowd, at the soundboard, directing the production. Unfortunately, on this night one particular spotlight operator either had a few too many beers or was hired only hours before the show. The spotlight was on when it was supposed to be off and vice versa through most of the show. Ted and the band members were lit at the completely wrong times. Can you imagine how exasperating it would be trying to talk to the audience in between songs in complete darkness? Well, it happened that night, and of course it's the performer, the one who's on stage, who really looks like the fool when the lights or sound are malfunctioning.

For forty years Ted has been a complete professional, never missing a concert, barely a lick, or even a pose. In 1978 political turmoil in a collapsed African country couldn't keep him from the infamous sold-out California Jam. When the small airport he was to depart from was closed, he trudged through swamps, avoided rebel gunfire, and commandeered a Red Cross relief plane out of Juba, Sudan. He flew to Cairo, then to London, and eventually made it to the Cal Jam stage via helicopter wearing the same soiled boots he'd had on in Africa.

Every commitment is important to Ted, and it is predominantly this working-hard attitude that he expects when he hires someone to do a job. Ted gives out instructions once. He's tough, but everyone knows all too well that only the best roadies can work for Ted Nugent. If he were a trapeze artist and needed to have someone catch him in the right place, at the same time, in every show, it would be no different. Anything else is failing miserably. Unfortunately, that's what we experience in our lives on almost a daily basis in one way or another. Needless to say, we got a new lighting director. Maybe it should have been me.

Fourteen years ago, I wouldn't have ever imagined doing what I did one night recently in London. It was incredibly bold, even given my rock-wife status, but during one concert I looked at my husband performing on stage, assessed the problem, and I just couldn't help myself.

We'd traveled to London for Ted and his band mates, Marco Mendoza and Tommy Clufetos, to perform concerts in England and Sweden. On the first night of the tour everyone expects a snafu or two,

Only highly regarded musicians and writers are invited to an annual gathering at the French country castle belonging to Sting's manager, Miles Copeland. Ted and I had planned that the three of us would travel to Paris together; then he would continue on to the castle while Rocco and I spent a few days going to museums and sight-seeing in Paris. Ultimately, we intended on meeting several days later in Cannes for some rest and family relaxation. Things were going so well with Ted at the castle, however, that everyone requested he extend his stay. Every day three different musicians like Carole King or Alannah Myles or writers like Desmond Childs (who is responsible for Ricky Martin's hits) would work together to create a song; by the end of the day they would record it right there on site. Ted was having fun and everyone loved his incredible talent for spontaneous input. He told me that if he passed by the studio and heard someone struggling with a guitar solo, he'd literally walk in, pick up a guitar, and say, "Try this." And blow them away. I, on the other hand, had my fill of traveling alone in a different country with a five-year-old in tow. I was ready to leave France and head for home if Ted couldn't join me in Cannes. Typically wives and family members are restricted from the songwriting workshop, but Rocco and I were eventually invited when everyone found out that Ted had promised to spend a family vacation with us. Staying in a real castle was certainly a treat for Rocco, and the people we were able to meet were very gracious and friendly. Ted's Damn Yankee partner Jack Blades has been an invited guest there, as well.

Although I realize I'm only one person, Ted has encouraged me to stand up for the things about which I am passionate, such as politics, the Second Amendment, my family, and anything that affects us. This strong, unyielding approach Ted has about life in general, and never giving in to anything that is second best, is truly the right approach. It's just sometimes hard to take when given out in the unsympathetic portions Ted heartily prepares. But then again, no one has ever accused my husband of being spineless. He is rarely undecided and often has more opinions than most people are willing to hear.

That's the joy of being Ted Nugent. He is obstinate and unwavering. He will never give up and never give in to corrupt politicians, animal rights activists, antigunners, or anyone who disagrees with him. This obviously makes our disagreements prohibitive, but I'm learning.

Ted, you may have guessed, has a small caliber of patience. Because we have so many other businesses with which to contend, there are always loose ends. At times it seems like Ted could unravel at any moment, although he never does. There are hundreds of requests for autographs every week, donations to charities, thousands of books to be signed, people who want "just a minute of his time," fellow hunters who steal his treestands, dogs that run away, cars and boats that don't start, foreigners who can barely speak English in charge of determining whether he's safe to fly, and foiled travel plans, just to name a few potential disruptions. Of course something is going to wind up broken when Ted wants to use it, or an important interviewer is going to call on one of our six home telephone lines when Ted has promised Rocco he'll play football with him.

This fast-paced lifestyle can be too overwhelming for many folks, even accomplished and highly organized ones. Much of the time, it's too much for me. We have myriad entities, and it's important to note that no one can do this single-handedly, either. Ted has an incredible team of competent, hardworking people around him that we lovingly refer to as TribeNuge—although he remains the one who makes the majority of the decisions. When one of us in the Tribe makes a mistake, however, we all hear about it.

Ted has little time to wait for people, anyone really, especially people driving in the left lane. Everything, it seems, begins and ends in the left lane. It's funny, but Ted often uses a person's driving skills as a gauge of character. People who drive slow in the left lane and are unaware that cars are lined up behind them are probably the type of people who go through life with a lackadaisical demeanor that will eventually get them in trouble. Criminals have indicated that they profile individuals who seem to have a similar carefree, unaware attitude. Maybe you're coming out of a mall and your arms are full of shopping bags and you forget where you parked your car. Maybe it's dark. Eventually you get lost. Chances are, you're ripe for the picking.

Ted amazes me with how aware he is of his surroundings 100 percent of the time; indeed, because he's never wanted to taint his senses, he's never touched a drug in his life. It is so important for my husband to be able to protect himself and his family, and to live in a country that allows us the freedom to defend ourselves is a predominant right that Ted has steadfastly been a proponent of for many years.

His political views landed him on the popular television show *Politically Incorrect* fifteen times. In fact, host Bill Maher emphatically stated that Ted was their number one most requested guest. There were times when the producers at *Politically Incorrect* called begging Ted to fly out for an upcoming show just when he'd returned from a lengthy tour or was gone on a hunting excursion, and he simply couldn't make the trip. But when he could, they always gave him the red-carpet treatment, sending first-class tickets for both Ted and me to fly out and putting us up in a beautiful five-star hotel in Los Angeles for days. Doing the show was indeed Ted's forte. He is one of the rare individuals who has actually grasped the true power of speech. He can speak to an auditorium full of kindergarteners, entertaining them and holding their attention just as well as he can to a room full of college grads, senior citizens, or FBI and police academy graduates. On several *Politically Incorrect* tapings, however, Ted told me that he felt he had to back down a bit to allow some of the other guests a chance to participate. After one show, he admitted he wished he hadn't. Very few people can debate with Ted and walk away thinking they had won. He was and is the master of debate.

Being the master, however, really does take a concerted effort. Ted's assistant, Linda Peterson, is an energetic professional who always makes things happen. Whenever something needs to be done and done right, whether it's Ted's travel arrangements or organizing schedules for Vice President Dan Quayle to visit the Ted Nugent United Sportsmen of America headquarters, Linda takes care of every last detail. She will take the time to notify Ted's hotel when he needs to have a wake-up call for a radio interview, for example, and even if it's three o'clock in the morning in her time zone, Linda will ring Ted's room (in addition to the wake-up call) to be certain that he's up. Weeks before the interview, Linda is on the phone with the radio people making arrangements so that when Ted telephones at a certain time he isn't made to wait on hold at an ungodly hour. (Believe it or not, it's happened—a lot!) Linda even confirms the talking points for the interview, because occasionally we run into disc jockeys who aren't all that experienced and aren't well versed on interview etiquette. Ted, of course, is every interviewer's dream and answers questions not in one or two words, but in one or two paragraphs. He could talk forever! This is one of the reasons why, several years ago, Ted broadcast his own morning radio show right out of our pole barn.

After he'd filled in for the WLLZ morning crew in Detroit that fall week of 1988 when we met, Ted hosted his own radio gab-and-jam fest each morning. A plethora of famous disc jockeys like Bob and Tom, Howard Stern, G. Gordon Liddy, Lewis and Floorwax, Oliver North, Mitch Albom, Larry King, and Rush Limbaugh had the opportunity to witness him in action. His sparkling wit and lightning-fast repertoire of facts about a wide range of topics—from apartheid to drug trafficking in Mexico to the best place to hunt antelope in North America—gave Ted the power to command audiences from coast to coast.

The Nuge radio show was a family affair, and Ted invited me to co-host on many occasions. In fact, when my diehard hunting hubby *chicken or tuna salad. Am I saying ya can't play ultimate guitar unless you hunt? Yes, I am.*

The spiritual erection lives. And the primal screams do erupt nonstop with teeth and hair and piss and gutpiles across attitude-driven America, have no doubt. At www.tednugent.com TalkBack, my own little American Spirit electrocommunication campfire, I am pleased by all the glowing attitude and goodwill shared by so many workin'-hard, playin'-hard soulbrothers and BloodBrothers out there. Does the spirit good. With a firebreathing rock-n-roll career that defies gravity, I deeply appreciate the energized support from so many for so long. I'm glad I'm not the only maniac out here. Though most correspondence is clearly inspired by people's desperate need to return to nature as healer and get back to the land as conscientious, hands-on resource stewards spurred on by my passion for the great outdoor and hunting lifestyle, I do get my fair share of inquiries about my greazy-ass R&B buttergritz-infested Gibson Byrdland guitarnoize. I currently stand tall on the mountaintop of fatherhood as my American Dream throbs on teaching my own children the gratifying joys of musical creativity on the ultimate instrument of expression—other than a 12-gauge riot shotgun—the mighty guitar, god of allthings R&B rock-n-roll. The Nuge stain is permanent, multigenerational, and eternally progressive. The road less traveled has twenty-two frets. Ride Sally, ride! Within that spectrum is uncharted territory that no whites have dared. Go there, ASAP.

Step number one—let the cleansing begin. I firmly believe that as goes the body, so goes the spirit, and if I have to abuse my eyes by taking in another vulgar glob of obesity runnin' amok in America, I think I'm gonna puke. If a person cannot manage his own body and soul better than the blubber-infested pigs groveling the streets of this land, then how the hell is he gonna discover the musical beast within? I ask you! Unless of course you've settled for playing country or western licks only, you must upgrade your overall quality of life in order to grasp and ultimately project the positives that churn forth from the corresponding positive attitude of reasonable self-worth. There's that wonderful attitude *word again. That's gonna keep resurfacing here, you watch.*

First off you're gonna need adequate weapons of mass destruction, American made of course. I recommend Gibson, Epiphone, Heritage, and Paul Reed Smith. They are wonderfully player-friendly. A good amplifier like a vintage Fender or any of the Peaveys out there is great. But whatever you do, do not load up on a bunch of effect pedals—in fact, none at all for starters. A direct, simple, clean signal with a cable between the guitar and the amp will teach you much about how accurately your personal guitar touch is developing, versus the artificial impression delivered by such effect pedals. This no-bullshit representation of your actual playing will go far as your own, personal musical visions begin to come on. Pedals and effects should augment your inner sound display, not create it in spite of yourself, and reliance on special effects can compromise the learning, development, and creative process. Wait as long as you can.

Surround yourself with every black record you can find. Essentials include every record by Howlin' Wolf, Lightnin' Hopkins, John Lee Hooker, Chuck Berry, Bo Diddley, James Brown, Wilson Pickett, Otis Redding, Sam & Dave, Elvis Presley, Booker T. & the MG's, all Motown recordings with The Funk Brothers on 'em, Link Wray, Lonnie Mack, the Ventures, Dick Dale & the Del-Tones, the first five albums by the Rolling Stones and the Beatles and the Yardbirds, the Jimi Hendrix collection, Van Halen, Stevie Ray Vaughn, and all my records to see how to implement all this soulful and sexual outrage into concise guitar patterns and songs. Then eat, sleep, drive, and shit with 'em all blaring into your skull as much as you can possibly stand it. Become one with the sonic beast.

Practice till ya puke. "I jammed everyday, I jammed everynight, I practiced till I knew all the licks. Now I'm on the verge of a nervous

Live big. Channel it from your intellectually stimulated mind, through your heart, into your guitar. Give a guitar to a kid. Jam hard. Look in the mirror and perfect that smile. Write a song called "Uncle Ted Jams Major Ass." Send me a copy of your tape. Eat massive BBQ. Scare all whites. Take no shit. Watch and study Braveheart, Schindler's List, Pearl Harbor, Saving Private Ryan, The Battle of the Bulge, The Green Berets, Cool Hand Luke, Bullitt, Deliverance, *and* The Patriot *over and over again and again. Be sure you know why we cannot go see concerts by Elvis Presley, Brian Jones, Jimi Hendrix, Mike Bloomfield, Janis Joplin, Jim Morrison, Canned Heat, Jerry Garcia, Bon Scott, John Belushi, and a whole slew of other stupid deadguys. Avoid their deathmarch lifestyles at all costs. Celebrate quality of life, truth, reality, health, a higher level of awareness, and the American Dream. Play guitar like ya mean it. Mean it. Spend maximum time around a fire with the ones you love. Celebrate the Spirit of the Wild daily.*

Although some may say that Ted's career is waning, few musicians have been fortunate enough to persevere in such a cannibalistic industry and continue to set records and sell out concerts even to this day as Ted has. Few rock musicians who ever made it big in the 1960s, '70s, '80s, or '90s continue to do anything other than play nightclubs, if they're lucky. Ted Nugent has the kind of staying power that keeps his booking agent busy every year, his manager in business, and me shopping at Neiman Marcus (only on occasion, of course). Musicians like Ted who have performed on TV every decade since the 1960s are rare. He's been called one of the greatest guitarists in the world. He's been deemed a virtuoso by friends Sammy Hagar and Eddie Van Halen. Ted doesn't let a machine play for him as many rap recording artists do today. Ted Nugent makes his own music. And doing so can be emotionally and physically demanding, especially on the road.

Raw Dogs and War Hogs

Even accomplishing ordinary tasks, like finding a dentist, can be a challenge when you're in a different city every day. On a recent tour Ted had four root canals within seven days all while continuing to perform two-hour-plus concerts. He never quits until he sucks out every last second of the day, and because he was on tour he also added four- to six-hour book signings for our just released and co-authored wild game cookbook, *Kill It & Grill It,* in every city, every day. It was phenomenal, really, and particularly enlightening to see record-setting lines of hundreds and even thousands of people waiting to get my husband's autograph at each Barnes & Noble or Borders bookstore. Certainly I was worried about my husband's health. There was only one other time that he had been in such physical pain.

Now that Ted and I have co-authored a wild game cookbook Kill It & Grill It, *I have been overwhelmed with the responsibility that comes along with signing my autograph next to Ted's. Parents don't look to drug addicts as role models for their children. They look to people of decency and goodwill, like my husband.*

Several years ago, when he was about to leave for a monthlong trip to Africa, Ted was doing the manly thing, cutting up a tree that had fallen down and blocked a favorite trail in our woods. He was using a chain saw when, in a split second, the blade sliced into his thigh. Only by God's will was he able to make the quarter of a mile to the house, crawl in the door, and call me for help. From the tone of his voice I understood the seriousness of the accident and ran downstairs to help him. In a matter of minutes I'd rushed him to a medical center where doctors stitched him up and, of course, encouraged him to delay his African safari. As you might guess, he didn't.

This recent problem with his root canal, however, was equally painful, maybe more, because something had gone terribly wrong. I knew it, and he knew it. There was never any relief from the persistent electrical-shock sensation he felt in his lower jaw in three weeks. Of course, no other human being could possibly keep the schedule Ted keeps and stay alive for more than a week. Thus I automatically jumped to conclusions and assumed that my husband wasn't getting enough rest, dismissing the possibility that a worse scenario had taken place. Neither Ted nor the doctors bought that rationalization. There must be something else, they agreed. Finally one doctor we visited in Houston said something to Ted that struck a chord, or a nerve. He said that the root canal had been done flawlessly; the x-ray showed that, and all the dentists Ted visited on the road confirmed it as well. There was only one other reason why Ted might be in agony. It was possible that one of the many doctors Ted had called upon while touring had inadvertently hit a nerve and done some damage. What scared me was what came next. If this was what had indeed happened, he told us, Ted would most likely feel that intense electrical sensation in his jaw—what had been keeping him awake every night for weeks—permanently!

"Let's get another opinion," I told Ted on the way out of the doctor's office. My throat was constricted and, had I let myself, I could have cried. Ted didn't need a whiny, whimpering wife, though. He needed me to be strong, so on the way back to the hotel, and in bed that night, I did some intense praying. Throughout our marriage I had seen God work some incredible miracles, and as you read through this book, you will read about how a divine force has helped me, and changed me dramatically over the years. That night in bed, even Ted asked me to pray for him. God works in mysterious ways!

Fortunately, Ted made it through the tour even though other musicians might have canceled their shows. It was, again, Ted's uncompromising constitution that kept him performing and continuing to give his audiences what they'd come for: a dynamic, fire-breathing, kick-ass rock-n-roll show. Only a few of us knew about the pain that Ted was enduring. Everyone said these concerts were the best shows of Ted's they'd ever seen. Even though I was slightly disappointed that Ted had left me in hard labor the night Rocco was born, because the show must go on. That is his makeup, his character.

LIVE IT UP

Most other tours have been fun and a fabulous opportunity for Ted, Rocco, and me to be together and travel the world. At times, of course, we just get moved along at a quicker-than-average pace and don't have a chance to see anything but airports and hotels. Still, basic needs like cleaning clothes must be met even while touring. I remember one particular time when Ted was on the KISS Farewell Tour during the summer of 2000; Rocco and I had been out on the road with Ted and the band for a couple of weeks, and because Ted always likes us to pack light, our clothes needed to be washed. When you're in a different city each day, it's often difficult to schedule time to fit in a trip to the hotel's washer and dryer, if it even has them. At one venue, however, I arranged to do my laundry backstage before, during, and after Ted's concert. In this case, the washer and dryer were located directly off the side of the stage, just beyond the ceiling-to-floor curtains that separate the band from the crew working behind the scenes. I threw my clothes in the washer and then rushed to the side of the stage to watch my husband perform. I switched the clothes to the dryer and went backstage to see my hubby and give him a big smooch after his set, then I returned to finish my laundry. Someone who wasn't completely paying attention left part of the curtains open, and while I was folding my underwear, I got to see KISS perform. I was watching Gene Simmons stick his tongue out and Paul Stanley swing from the rafters. It was kind of surreal, but that's the life of a rock-n-roll wife.

Touring is more rigorous than most people would care to know. Many just choose to believe that it's always glamorous, and yes, there are times when it *is!* There are many occasions, however, when the tedium can seem endless. Traveling to a different city every day while on tour is a necessity. Any musician who has had the opportunity to work with Ted knows that he *rarely* enjoys a day off, so unless there is a show two nights in a row in any particular city, the band and crew often work and travel seven days a week. *The Motor City Madman is a workaholic!*

With nearly every sunrise, the band and crew see a new hotel and concert facility, and because of that it's not unusual to forget the hotel room number, which both Ted and I have managed to do several times. On one occasion we took a four-hour tour bus ride after a concert and meandered into the hotel long before the birds were awake. Ted's faithful and experienced tour manager, Bobby Quandt, escorted us into the hotel elevator and took us directly to our room, opened the door, and had our bags delivered. We were so tired that we immediately went to sleep. The next morning we got up, grabbed our room keys, and headed for the nearest Starbucks. For security purposes, the room numbers are rarely printed on the room keys, so after we got our java jolt, we headed back to our room and quickly realized neither one of us knew our room number. With Bobby taking such good care of us and guiding us to our room while we were half asleep, we'd just forgotten to look at the number on the door. To add to the confusion, Ted (along with many other celebrities) registers his room under secret names to evade diehard fans. Fortunately the front-desk personnel recognized Ted and gave us our room number.

On another occasion I quietly slipped out of the room early one morning (so Ted and Rocco could sleep longer) and went in-line skating. It wasn't until after I exited the hotel and rounded two corners that I realized I didn't even know the name of our hotel. Thankfully (I thought), Ted was touring with KISS. I saw the KISS crew getting off their bus and I assumed we were staying together. To my embarrassment, I eventually discovered we weren't even staying at the same hotel. Ours was a mile away. I was lost, tired, and not very skilled on my skates. Then I had to convince the front-desk clerk that I really was Mrs. Ted Nugent, although we weren't registered under that name.

Thoughtful Interjection: *If you really are a diehard fan and happen to know where your favorite musician is staying, consider this: Do you honestly think your idol is going to open the door to a complete stranger and invite you into his room? Most of these guys really need their rest and don't care to be bothered in their hotel rooms.*

Sleep is a rare but very welcome commodity in the life of a rock star. Like most highly energized musicians, Ted usually has a difficult time sleeping on the road. Long after he exits the stage his mind is racing with new music ideas and plans for making the tour run smoothly. Travel can and usually does interrupt sleep patterns, especially when concerts are played in different time zones one day after the next. It's important for employees, family members, and friends to acknowledge these vicissitudes. Ted has had telephone calls from well-meaning friends at eight o'clock in the morning after getting off the stage well after midnight and getting to sleep at three. The fact is, it's hard for him to get excited when he hears from that old hunting buddy at the crack of dawn.

Although Ted has been known for his strictly regimented lifestyle and often imposes his restrictive demands upon those around him, he is also extraordinarily generous. On the KISS tour, there was a day off between shows when all of the crew buses were to travel within fifty miles of home. Of course, Ted opened up our home and private heaven-on-earth property (by this time a thousand acres) to the entire KISS Farewell band and entourage for a big wild game Nuge Bash barbecue. With Ted keeping a skeleton crew of about five guys, the opening act's band and crew, and the KISS crew and ours, we had about fifty rock-dog guests at our home that day, and we had a blast. Since everyone works mostly night shifts, it was like watching vampires come out during the day with squinting eyes. A Nugent party wouldn't be a party without firepower, so we had extra Jet Skis brought in to our private lake, skeet shooting on our private range, and, of course, lots of venison backstrap on the grill. The highlight of the day, however, was watching Ace Frehley slowly, almost painstakingly meander over to Ted at the gun range and ask if he could shoot. The looks on the faces of the crew were priceless. They all ran for cover and hid behind trees and a couple of trucks that were nearby. Ted had flawlessly demonstrated how milk jugs filled with red water can be blown up at superswift speeds—and the crowd went "Oh!" And then he allowed Ace to lean up against him for support. Now, everyone who had originally gathered around the shooting range to watch Ted's quick-draw shooting techniques was fifty to seventy yards away, fearing Ace wasn't all that stable, but he surprised us all. He was actually a darn good shot.

On the KISS tour, I never had much of a chance to get to know Ace, but he was always kind to Rocco and me, which is greatly appreciated. Peter Criss and his wife, Gigi, were especially nice and friendly to us. And when Ted first introduced Rocco and me to Gene Simmons and Paul Stanley in their dressing room, they both stopped what they were doing to talk to Rocco and ask him about sports and the latest Pokémon. While we could have been met with a cold and unfriendly reception, Gene, Paul, Peter, and Ace all made us feel like a welcome part of the KISS Farewell Tour. *(Gene tried to make me feel a little* too *welcome . . . more on that later!)*

Since the musicians must allow themselves the liberty of practicing their instruments daily, it is nearly impossible for them to be well informed on every aspect of the tour, including finances. Several of Ted's rock-dog cronies leave most of their financial responsibilities to accountants and business managers. Few of them actually take an active role in determining how every dime is spent. Working musicians are either in the recording studio or on the road. *Constantly.* They have little time to review detailed financial reports, which obviously leaves them wide open to a whole lot of abusive situations. People can and do take advantage of anyone who has money because in some unimaginable, unjustifiably wicked way, they rationalize their taking a piece of the action. They think that since a celebrity or someone who has simply worked hard has an abundance of financial resources (that is, more than *they* have), then there must be a little excess for them, and they end up swindling some cash here or there. It happens and happens often. People, sometimes those you think you know and trust the most, will steal either time or money from you.

In the late 1970s when Ted was the biggest touring act in the world, selling out stadiums like Madison Square Garden and the California Jam hundreds of nights a year, he made a startling discovery about his finances. When there should have been tens of millions of dollars in the bank, he discovered that the man who'd acted as both his business manager and attorney had mismanaged his assets, leaving a huge dent in his bank account. In fact, his chief executive officer had left him in debt instead of in the black. This guy was apparently living the high life while Ted was busy touring and recording and being Ted—the most frugal man in the world, saving thirty-cent receipts for tolls. At one time Ted was the proud owner of world-famous, award-winning Clydesdale horses along with the largest mink ranch in North America. He should have been able to buy anything he wanted anytime he wanted to buy it. He should have lived in the most elaborate house, with an enormous built-in swimming pool, with a guest house and maybe a sauna or two. In an average night's work, Ted could bring home anywhere from one hundred thousand to five hundred thousand dollars—and that was in the seventies. Sad thing was, he hardly spent a dime, which was just his nature. His hard-earned fortune was literally pissed away by rotten business management. Ted lived in the same modest ranch house for twenty years, wore practically the same clothes, and rarely bought anything unnecessarily elaborate. He did own a Corvette, but that, of course, was a utilitarian method of transportation for Ted.

When I married my husband in 1989, I'm proud to say it wasn't for money. Ted wasn't the biggest touring act in North America. He was busy getting the Internal Revenue Service off his back, digging out of the black hole into which some incompetent attorney had dumped him. He was selling valuable tracts of land, eight-by-ten glossy photographs, and vintage guitars, along with, of course, continuing his quest to make music.

This might also be the reason why Ted has never slowed down and never stopped burning too many irons in the fire. Because of that, the business of *this* rock star is quite unlike that of any other. As Ted wrote in his recent song "Crave,"

A simple life I will not have
It doesn't satisfy me
I don't believe in the status quo
It kinda leaves me weak
A mountain high is what I climb,
I swim the river deep,
And if ya crave the time of your life, try to keep up with me.
I'm gonna live
I'm gonna fly
I'm gonna soar till the day I die.
On the wings of a Byrd of prey, hey, hey, hey,
You're absolutely what I crave.
Look at me that's a smile on my face.
You know it don't come cheap.
Sure I live the American Dream, go ahead and crucify me.

These lyrics best describe Ted's *in-your-face* attitude and also why he's been able to maintain a viable career—*several* viable careers, actually—for more than forty years. He's going to do whatever he wants, when he wants to do it. Now, however, we scrutinize our books much more diligently.

"And if a house gets in my way I'll burn it down" ("Stranglehold")

When many might have just licked their wounds and spent the remainder of their lives playing nightclub gigs, Ted, never being satisfied with settling down, continued to release albums that may not have been huge commercial successes, but allowed him the opportunity to keep making music for his diehard fans and tour nearly nonstop. Ted, being more of a creative species, has always been too busy, totally consumed in his music or hunting operations to have the time (or desire) to become overly immersed in his finances, or to look at numbers. Considering what has happened to him in the past, though, my husband has kindly insisted that I take on a more aggressive role managing our finances over the years.

It wasn't always that way. In the beginning of our married life, when I began the daunting task of paying the bills, I was unfamiliar with what economic responsibilities were required of a rock star. How much exactly did pyrotechnics cost at a show? Ten thousand a night? Twenty? So here I was making constant inquiries to Ted's current manager, Doug Banker (who was responsible for discovering that Ted's former manager-attorney had bilked him for tons of cash), about exactly what needed to be paid, and why, which I don't think he really appreciated all that much. Who would? Your long-term client's new, twenty-six-year-old wife is suddenly calling *you,* the manager, curious as to why we couldn't just use another insurance company and save money. That was my duty, really, to seek out the best deals for everything. The amount of time and effort that goes into the business of managing a rock-n-roll musician is unimaginable. Someone has to calculate and monitor every time one of his songs is played on the radio or used in a movie. Then every person in the band who ever received a portion of the songwriting royalty must get paid. To this day I still cut checks to guys who were in Ted's band twenty-five years ago.

Eventually I learned that putting on a concert was a business just like anything else. It was shocking to me that even after Ted's 1980s management scam, he still didn't scrutinize the expense report, but that is Ted's fatal flaw: He trusts people. Since he fulfills all of his commitments, he assumes that others will, as well. Because of this, I've had to become the bad guy. Like a mother bear protecting her cubs, I sometimes think that everyone is out to get my husband and I'm constantly on the lookout for swindlers. Things are settling down, though. Along with Ted's current manager and an incredibly loyal and industrious bookkeeping assistant, Kevin, we have kept Ted's management and accounting team on their toes.

Managing a rock star is a whole different ball game, and Ted must be either the easiest or the most complex client for whom any decent manager could ask. Compared to namby-pamby rock-n-roll divas who make unrealistic demands like taking out all the brown M&Ms backstage (this really happened), Ted is pretty straightforward. He doesn't ask for a lot. His rider—the contract in which the artist and crew request a list of food and goodies backstage at each concert—is very basic. Most concert promoters and facilities are locked in to supplying whatever the musicians want, so they can demand just about anything, and often do. From what I've heard, only a small number of bands abuse this privilege. Other than a few beers for the crew, there is no alcohol backstage at Ted's shows, and certainly no smoking. Anyone who's ever been within two feet of Ted and had a cigarette dangling from his mouth can confirm how much he despises that proven cancer-causing smoke. With a taunting, scornful smile Ted will lean in close and ask, "What do you want me to tell your kids at your funeral? You didn't love them?" People would smile, but you knew they got the message. Ted always makes a point with his bold, dynamic presence.

Thankfully, our fabulous road manager Bob Quandt takes care of literally every last detail of the tour while Ted is on the road. Bobby and I communicate several times a day about everything from deposits to travel arrangements to lighting or even making Ted a dentist appointment. It all can get very complicated.

In the meantime, while Ted can be performing in St. Louis, I might be back at home on a telephone conference with our banker and accountant. Being a rock star's wife, I discovered, is a full-time job.

Back at home, the Ted Nugent United Sportsmen of America empire was running at full bore, and nearly out of control. We hadn't really planned on doing so many things at the same time, and with Ted on the road, some details were neglected. There were so many things that needed immediate attention *from him,* and when he wasn't available for input, our staff made the best decisions they could. A newsletter evolved into a magazine, and suddenly a nonprofit Kamp for Kids seemed like a terrific idea. What we needed was ten more people on the payroll to help, but that was never an option. Ted and I have never made a profit from the hunting business. Although the company grossed millions over the years, it all ended up right back in the business of promoting our hunting and gun rights, and what didn't went into corrupt employees' pockets. We caught more than a dozen employees stealing from us during a decade. *Another headache.*

Around that same time I had found a niche in our small rural Michigan community and opened my own aerobics studio, feeling the need to stay in shape. As a certified professional fitness instructor, I was quite busy teaching classes, managing our other businesses, and of course raising Rocco. Ted was intrigued by an offer from a fellow hunter who wanted to produce a satellite television show for him, and knowing that I was too busy he went along with this guy's program. Ted, I assumed, could handle the details and would ask if he needed my editing or videography assistance, since I did have production experience from my days at the University of Florida and Wayne State

Early in our marriage I realized that I could either wave good-bye to my husband or join in his hunting adventures. When I finally grasped that there were not only legal and ethical but also religious reasons to hunt, I couldn't deny justifying it. A passage from the Bible reads, "Take thy quiver and thy bow and get me some venison" (Genesis 27:3). As Ted says: "Sir, yes, Sir!" And also, "Every moving thing that liveth shall be meat for you" (Genesis 9:3), to which Ted responds, "No shit!"

I always thought that the American dream meant to work hard and reap the rewards of your efforts. Apparently some individuals in the outdoor industry seem to think otherwise, at least about Ted. While other television personalities can have sucessful programs, my husband is, from time to time criticized for having any desire beyond using his rock-n-roll income to finance his hunting business. It's sad to me, because Ted's only desire is to get the message out to the non-hunting public to help safeguard the shooting and hunting sports for generations to come. Ted has sold millions of albums, had a New York Times *best-selling book, and can reach across the border into the mainstream media and on almost any nationally syndicated radio or TV show or newspaper, all to promote the truth about conservation and our Second Amendment rights.*

Queen of the Forest

My fatal flaw in life, it seems, is that I usually take things one step farther than I really should. In 1998, at Ted's urging, I started a nonprofit organization called Queen of the Forest, which is designed to educate and empower women about the spirituality of the great outdoors. Ted, I think, had something else in mind when he suggested I put together an all-women's hunt, but the more I thought about it, the more I realized that there were a lot of women like me who didn't really understand the truth about hunting and wildlife management. My goal was to reach the nonhunting women, a vast audience that could easily be swayed by animal rights propaganda. It was never my intention to turn as many women into hunters as possible. Not at all. In fact, I realized that some women would attend the weekend-long Queen of the Forest clinics only because their boyfriends, husbands, fathers, sons, or brothers coerced them. During one camp, at the beginning when I introduce the staff and myself, review the agenda, and then ask all the women why they've come, I noticed that one of the girls wasn't all that enthused. Surprisingly, I had an animal rights activist in camp! She had come to see what it was that I did at the Queen of the Forest camp and was pretty intent that she was not going to have a good time. My work was cut out for me. I had never anticipated this, but I just prayed and stuck to the agenda, which was jam-packed with activities that were important to every woman, not just hunters specifically.

We teach self-defense, fitness, nutrition, survival skills, basic archery, wildlife history, and handgun training. At the break of dawn and at sunset, we put every woman in a tree stand or a ground blind and let nature unfold. They see North American bison, white-tailed deer, wild sheep, wild Russian boar, and, of course, more squirrels and birds and ducks and geese than they've probably ever had the opportunity to see in their lives. We breathe fresh, crisp air and bask in the warm glow of a slow sunset while maple leaves gently spiral to the forest floor all around us.

At the end of the weekend the animal rights gal was actually crying, and when I asked why, she hugged me and said that she'd experienced a life-changing event. Many of them do. I take them to the mountaintop. We soar on the wings of an eagle. We don't talk about gut piles and hunting. We talk about the spiritual connection we have with Mother Nature. We try to solve each other's problems. We laugh.

Chapter Four

Stormtroopin'—The Politics of Rock-n-Roll

May 13, 2002

OUR ALARM FAILED TO WAKE US AT 5:00 A.M., BUT our faithful caretaker/kamikaze warrior employee Jim Lawson arrived at 5:30 to pick us up for the airport. We grabbed our suitcases and left for the *Kill It & Grill It* press tour in five minutes flat. Once in Washington, D.C., we never stopped. A driver was waiting for us at the airport and took us to a dozen different interviews that day, including CNN *Crossfire,* Oliver North, G. Gordon Liddy, and Greta Van Susteren. My broadcasting background came in handy when these tenacious talk-show hosts fired off question after question about everything from our hunting lifestyle to our political views. The hardest part for me was finding a gap in Ted's dialogue. Ted's passion for the Second Amendment and our hunting lifestyle is resolute, so it's quite difficult to get a word in, but I managed to do so once or twice. He bases his opinions on facts and that blows people away. I've yet to witness anyone who brings intelligent conversation to the table come close to shutting him down. It's beautiful. He makes sense and I think people are most amazed that a man with a ponytail can beat them at their own games. I love watching him in action, but even more, I love being a part of the banter. From time to time I miss working in radio and television, and it feels good to be able to get back into the ring now and then on major media programs.

It was 11:30 P.M. before Ted and I returned to the Mayflower Hotel, ordered soup, and crashed. The next morning we woke up before dawn again for a New York City shuttle for more press with our old pals from Fox—the dynamic duo, Sean Hannity and Alan Colmes, entertainment TV shows, and dozens of nationally syndicated radio shows. Everyone seemed fascinated with the concept of killing one's own sustenance, where it is simply a way of life for us. Every day I pull out a package of meat that has the date the animal was harvested. We eat only what we kill, with the exception of a leg of lamb on Easter, or Amish turkey when it's not turkey season.

Going Down Hard

They called me "white trash," and "whore," and "slut." Me! A former Catholic schoolgirl and high school cheerleader. The animal rights activists Ted and I encountered in San Francisco that day were more than just verbally abusive. Their body language became frighteningly unnerving as they taunted us with expletives. It was like a movie scene where I was watching someone get harassed, and she was about to be stabbed. That's how I felt.

It was a comfortable but cool and sunny Sunday in northern California, and Ted actually had a day off from his tour, which was rare. As he and I strolled hand and hand down the garbage- and bum-laden streets of San Francisco, I remember thinking how safe I felt in secure environment, all because they want to impose their illogical convictions on the world. Hunters don't threaten vegetarians. Animal rights activists don't seem to want to listen to the fact that wildlife management is necessary for us to live in this world. We keep building more and more houses and malls and expect the orphaned animals to nest—*where?* We push them aside to build highways and golf courses and then get angry because the geese droppings clutter the sidewalks. Even I would have welcomed the opportunity to talk to these people, one on one, to try to explain the facts, but they just didn't want to listen to me, Ted, or anyone. I guess they prefer to be violent and verbally confrontational.

All of that entered my mind as we passed the protestors and walked into Neiman Marcus. This time, their verbal threats escalated to the point that I was concerned about leaving the safety of the store. At what point does a lunatic make his move? Whenever opportunity arises. And there he was, six foot two and ponytailed, their archenemy in the flesh. *Mr. Opportunity.* This was their chance to get Ted. It was the moment for which they had been waiting, a moment in which I was acutely aware.

My shopping was hurried and served only as a minor distraction from what was waiting for us outside the door. Of course, I was uneasy about another confrontation, but Ted wasn't worried. In fact, while I browsed through the store, he actually went back outside to talk with law enforcement officers standing guard to make sure that the protest remained peaceful. Later, we discovered that these protests occurred every Sunday afternoon and had caused hundreds of thousands of dollars in damage to the Neiman Marcus store just a few months earlier. One of the head protestors was already convicted of throwing rocks through Neiman's plate glass windows in demonstration of his disapproval of the fur salon. Nice guy.

Finally it was time to go, and the sad part of this story is that Ted said he'd actually thought about buying me a fur coat so I could walk out of the store and tempt the antis even further. Darn! I should have pursued that! In any event, we exited the building into the snarling rants of the animal rights protestors, and this is when the trouble began.

Now, it seemed, I was the target. Ted, of course, was recognizable and quite a bit more outspoken than I had ever been in regard to hunting, trapping, and eating animal flesh. I've never *demanded* that anyone do what I do or live the way I do, should their lifestyle choices differ from mine. My carefully planned Queen of the Forest programs never force-fed the concept of hunting. I realize that some of us inherently do not enjoy the actual killing of animals, but it is important that we understand the necessity of managing the precious, renewable resource that is wildlife, especially if we choose to eat meat and wear leather products, or even live on this planet.

One of the protestors, dressed in ripped and dirty clothing, was now in my face screaming at the top of her lungs. With her tattered hip huggers slouching about five miles below her navel, she called me "white trash" over and over as Ted grabbed my hand and pulled me closer. It was disconcerting as all hell to endure these taunting assaults. I actually began to feel sick inside and became aware that their verbal attacks were getting to me. Now a whole group of people began to swarm around us. For the first time, Ted, who was still smiling although they called him equally enraging names, told me not to let their outlandish allegations bother me. Easier said than done. To my surprise, Ted was the cool-headed one, handling the vehement thundering from their troops very well. He smiled casually and asked them to leave us alone several times as we began walking away from the six or eight protestors who began to descend upon us.

What one particular woman said to me was blasphemous and began to make me physically upset. This tattered-looking hippie leaned right into my face and called me "slut," and then added, "How much do you get paid, honey?" For some stupid reason, I couldn't respond. My whole body froze like some sort of bad less trusting, not more to these potential enemy forces that supposedly come to seek asylum. Excuse me, but we Americans need asylum now.

Since the attack, I have seen a new energy in many people who are saying the same things my husband has been saying for years. Grandmothers, schoolteachers, police officers, and ministers are speaking out in complete support of defending our country and destroying evil. But I was astounded the other day, when I went into a local coffee shop where dozens of people, mostly senior citizens, were gathering early one morning for breakfast. All around me, there were intense conversations, all focusing on the plane crashes. Then a demure, weathered, and well-respected woman began pounding her fist on the table. The entire restaurant grew silent and everyone turned to look at her as this petite, white-haired pistol stood up and shouted, "Bush should just nuke the bastard!"

Earth Tones

It was a freezing winter day in Saginaw, Michigan, and Ted had just finished his sound check, but I don't remember if my bones were shaking from the cold or from the unthinkable challenge Ted was about to face. A few months earlier, my husband had received a letter from a distressed man who was desperately trying to get his nephew, a huge Ted Nugent fan, to stop drinking, and wondered if Ted might be able to help. The kid was young, fourteen, and had been excited to go on his first hunting trip with his father, but this hunting story did not have a happy ending. The father placed his son in a treestand, wished him luck, and told him he would be back at dark to get him. The two men had eagerly anticipated that first Opening Day for years, I was told, both being dedicated hunters looking forward to the white-tailed deer season when the son was finally legally old enough to hunt with a bow and arrow. It was a day that they would remember forever and would surely bring them closer together, as well. When dusk set in, however, the father approached his son's treestand and the son, overly excited, drew his bow and arrow and aimed at the thick, dark gray mass that moved between the trees—thinking, of course, it was a deer. He shot, and soon realized that he had shot his own father.

So here was this young man, standing backstage all torn up inside with emotions I could never fathom. A year had passed since his father's death, maybe two. He had been drinking and doing drugs, and his family was concerned about him. They had tried several drug and alcohol intervention programs but nothing seemed to help this kid. As Ted and I walked hand in hand down the cold, sterile, concrete hallway, I wondered what my husband could say to this kid that would make him stop drinking or even help him move on with his life. What a daunting task. My hands began to sweat and my body would not stop shivering.

We entered a small room off the hallway where the uncle who'd initially contacted Ted was waiting along with a few other relatives including the boy's mother. The young man, who appeared to be at least a little bit drunk or high, was also there. His eyes had that half-opened, half-closed look. The uncle thanked Ted for coming, a few people exchanged hellos, and I was a nervous wreck. My insides were flipflopping. What could you possibly say to a young man who had killed his own dad on their first hunt together to make him see that drinking didn't really solve any problems? It didn't bring his father back and it wouldn't improve the quality of his life. He was too young to be going through this, and I felt so horrible for him, his family, and now for Ted. But somehow, I knew that my husband would say the right thing.

With the most gallant sense of power a human being could summon, my husband approached this juvenile, a young man who made a poor choice that cost him his whole world, and did something that stunned us all. He grabbed the boy, who was half sitting, half resting on the edge of a table, by the collar of his shirt, and with an icy gaze pulled the kid up and made him look him straight in the eyes. That poor kid's eyes sprang open fast, as did mine and everyone else's.

"Do you think your dad would have wanted you to be drinking?" Ted snapped at the young, astonished kid, who now was so shocked that he could only slightly move his head from right to left. The room had grown quiet enough that you could hear the noise of the kid's clothing scratching as it moved in opposite directions.

"I know what happened was horrible. I know you made a terrible mistake. I know you're sorry," Ted said, never wavering from within an inch of this kid's face, never losing eye contact. Never losing intensity, but lowering his tone somewhat, Ted said, "But now it's time to move on."

There was a long pause.

I remember feeling the weight of that poor kid's life on my shoulders. I felt as though I was somehow experiencing what he had endured; or maybe it was just that I was becoming so close to Ted now that I felt what he felt.

"Learn from this, kid. Look over there at your family."

The boy's mother was crying, as she probably had been for a while, years maybe. She'd not only lost a husband, but lost a son, as well.

"They love you and care about you. *You!* And you're breaking their hearts. You still have your whole life in front of you. You're one of the lucky ones. Yeah, that's right. Just today I talked with a young kid maybe about your age, his name is Chip Stewart, and he has a terrible disease through no fault of his own. He's in a wheelchair and couldn't move his legs if he wanted to. And look at you. You're throwing away all God's gifts. Chip would give his left nut to have one more week in your shoes, walking through the woods, hunting, running, and dancing. He's slowly losing all of his motor skills and soon he won't even be able to hug his mother. When was the last time you hugged yours?" The kid just looked down. "Hey? I'm up here. Go hug your mother and tell her how much you love her 'cause you may not have another chance to do it. In fact, you'll probably forget," Ted commanded like a drill sergeant. And the young man did as he said.

My heart felt a sigh of relief and I wiped the tears that rolled down my cheeks. Just today I received an e-mail from Chip, as I do almost every day. Ted and I have kept in touch with him over the years and have even brought him to our home for a sacred hunt with the Motor City Madman. It was heart-wrenching to watch Ted carry Chip up and down our staircase and onto the four-wheelers, but neither of them seemed to care. We'd promised Chip a git-down with Uncle Ted and that's what he got. Bless his heart. Chip has Friedreich's ataxia. It's a progressive neuromuscular disorder that affects motor skills. The disease usually begins at puberty and progresses for the remainder of the patient's life, but sometimes symptoms may not show up until later in life. It is a slow progression. So maybe it isn't all that difficult for Ted to speak with young, wayward teens after watching friends like Chip enduring real pressure. Chip's spirit and attitude inspire us immensely. We call him "Blood Brother."

Ted continued his talk with the troubled youth and lessened his chokehold on him mentally. Eventually my husband changed the tune and had the kid and everyone else in the room laughing. A huge tidal wave of pain had been lifted from that family. Ted had made his point and it took guts, power, and tenacity to be able to even think about approaching another human being in that way, but it transformed that kid's life. He was able to stop drinking and realize that what the Motor City Madman, his idol, had said to him that night actually made sense. It took a rock-n-roll guitar player, not a counselor, a police officer, a minister, or a doctor, but a guitar player to figure out that one.

Ted Nugent has changed a lot of people's lives. And it is this very same influence that has gained him recognition on prominent news programs such as Fox News's *Hannity & Colmes,* Greta Van Susteren, CNN's *Crossfire,* Court TV, and many more. In fact, Ted could make monthly or even weekly appearances on a number of shows if he had the time. His assistant, Linda, is inundated with requests from TV news producers who are all too eager to get Ted's comments on anything from his music to the National Rifle Association. It seems as though whenever a new gun law is proposed, the media calls Ted for his interpretation. Unfortunately, however, the NRA and some of Ted's own cohorts can't always grasp his media wizardry.

KLUSTRPHNKY

Ten years ago Ted and I were invited to attend a Safari Club International Awards banquet where we were the guests of honor and received an award. It truly was an honor for me, because I had not been in the hunting industry as long as Ted, and only recently began my undertaking as an outdoor writer and associate editor of our *Ted Nugent Adventure Outdoors* magazine. Hundreds of people came up to us, excited to meet Ted, and after a wild game dinner he gave an impromptu speech about how all sportsmen and -women could do more for the outdoors by getting women and kids involved to help safeguard the sport for future generations. Most people don't realize that Ted is actually a comedian. He is such a dynamic and eloquent speaker but will quickly change gears and have you rolling on the floor laughing. That night he received a standing ovation, as he usually does, and while he was signing autographs I quietly excused myself and ventured to the rest room unnoticed. Coming back, I made my way from the back door of the ballroom forward, as all eyes, or most of them, were focused on my husband. A long line snaked around the large room where people stood stoically with eight-by-ten photographs, albums, bows, arrows, guns, and even guitars for Ted to sign. For hours he sat there patiently, smiling, signing them all, stopping momentarily to talk with little girls or boys and ask them when they were going to go hunting. He would ask everyone where they were from or at least how they were doing that evening. Ted was and is very personable.

A couple of gentlemen were still sitting at a table I was about to pass and I couldn't help but hear their conversation as I walked by their table.

"What's with the '*whack 'em and stack 'em*' crap?" one middle-aged man asked another man as they both chugged beers and smoked. "What a loser. He can't say that shit. The antis will be all over him, and us." The other man shook his head and said, "Yeah, he just gives hunting a bad name." The two men never saw me walk by. But later I saw them in line, and they asked Ted to sign a few photos and said they were big fans.

It's difficult to deny that Ted has influenced hundreds of people through our Ted Nugent United Sportsmen of America organization, tednugent.com, where he communicates almost daily with people from all over the world on the TalkBack boards, and through the vast number of radio, television, and newspaper interviews he conducts to appeal to people to lead sober lives, introducing thousands of people to shooting, hunting, and other outdoor sports. Surprisingly, however, it is from within this very rank-and-file that Ted receives undue criticism, even after providing the hunting establishment with an entirely new mainstream audience that no other high-profile individuals could reach. It appears to be nothing other than disorderly conduct. Here is a man who has the wherewithal to encourage more nonhunters to support the outdoor manufacturers—that is, spend money—but is sometimes shot down with unfounded criticism about his ponytail. He is a Drug Abuse Resistance and Education (DARE) officer and spokesperson for Mothers Against Drunk Driving (MADD). On any given travel day at an airport, truck stop, restaurant, or school we meet all types of people who stop Ted to thank him for speaking out about the Second Amendment and hunters' rights—Navy SEALs, cops, marines, fighter-jet pilots, farmers, mechanics, welders, military heroes, ranchers, truck drivers, lawyers, CEOs, doctors, federal marshals, mayors, representatives, senators, governors, grandmothers, grandfathers, moms, dads, sons, daughters, other celebrities like Bob Seger and Alice Cooper—nearly every type of person, tall, short, big, little, African American, Asian, Native American, acknowledge his hard work. Although it's tough, sometimes, to be on time for our plane, it makes my spirit soar, and Ted's too, to see that his efforts are noticeable to the masses. At his official hometown Texas barbecue inaugural, President George W. Bush said, "Thanks for coming, Ted," and leaned in close to his cheek. "You're a good man."

Without a doubt, most shooting sports industry members show their overwhelming appreciation of Ted's presence and recognize his ability to open doors to the nonhunting public. Sure, my husband has made some mistakes, and if you ask me, I think he swears too much, but I don't think Secretary of Health and Human Services Tommy Thompson, Homeland Security Director Tom Ridge, or Michigan Governor John Engler would call just anybody at home, do you?

There's been some controversy over the years about glorifying the kill and whether Ted's "whack 'em and stack 'em" theme has caused some conflict within the hunting community. Well, I'll be honest, before I met Ted, I'll admit, I didn't want to hear about how my dinner had to die. Like many others, I don't like to discuss blood and guts. I don't like the thought of taking a life, any life—even a frog's. But I didn't really care for giving birth either, if you want to know the truth. It hurt like hell. I thought I was dying. I had a forty-five-hour labor with *no* drugs! What could be fun about that? Nothing.

News flash: During the actual moment of birth or death there is pain.

Yes, there are those who disagree, those who have no conscience at all. There are also death-row inmates and people who rob, rape, and murder. They can separate the feelings of pain, discomfort, and even joy from which taking a life and making a life evolve.

Even our hometown newspaper, which publishes a biweekly Ted Nugent article, printed a letter to the editor attacking their own celebrity writer. It read, "The thing I find most troubling is [Ted's] orgasmic response to killing something." *Orgasmic?* Hardly (and I can attest to that!) But yes, I would say that Ted is very happy, even elated, when he harvests an animal and provides sustenance for our family. Certainly this critic and most others have relished a delectable piece of meat that was so tender it fell off the bone, or a scrumptious lobster bisque, or a luscious turkey dinner enjoyed with family and friends at Thanksgiving. I wonder if this person had ever hummed "*mmm*" whenever eating a delicious piece of animal flesh. Yes, even that hot dog at the baseball park has *some* animal parts. Although it happens, it is rare to live in America and be raised without having enjoyed animal protein at some point. Anyone who has pressed a knife into a slab of steak, jabbed his fork into the meat, and chewed has enjoyed and delighted in the killing process, as well. Several friends of mine hate to admit it when my husband broaches the subject, but even the tuna for their salads spent two days gagging to death on the way to the can.

Whether or not we will recognize it, we are all responsible for the death of the billions of chickens that are bought and sold at fast-food restaurants daily. There are too many people, however, who want to conveniently disassociate themselves from the actual kill. They don't want to acknowledge the death of a living, breathing entity. I can understand that. It's one of the reasons hospitals have waiting rooms. If you saw your loved one cut open, being operated on, and then sewn back together, it would probably make you sick. If, at some point, it didn't, I'd have to think that there's something wrong with you. Most of us connect on a deep level with the feeling of pain, even for others. In a way, we all feel pain for taking the life of an animal. Yes, even big, bad hunters do too. And if they didn't, I would say they're either lying or *big, bad hunters.*

But death is part of life (along with taxes, but that's another sad story!). No one really likes to talk about it, but death happens every day. You can't live on this earth without partaking in the actual feat of killing something. The house you live in, the roads you drive on, even your vegetable gardens were the comfortable homes of trillions of animals, birds, and insects. All the animal rights activists who choose to believe that *they* are somehow better than those of us who prefer to eat meat and serve our children milk with cookies are missing out on a big piece of this puzzle. America is the land of the free, last time I checked.

Whether or not you own up to the fact that even your presence on this planet has displaced millions of animals and you, in fact, are responsible for killing animals, the truth is, hunters or not, we have all been liable for death in the animal kingdom. Hunters, I believe, are just more honest about what they do, the food they bring to the table, and yes, even the passion they have for their actions. Many misunderstand the enthusiasm that people like Ted express when they take a life. I can tell you that he is genuinely angry and upset whenever an animal is wounded. However, this happens to less than 1 percent of animals harvested. More often, Ted, and many other good, responsible hunters execute quick, humane kills. For this they are grateful.

Kill is a tough word to swallow. It's harsh. It's seemingly cold and hateful. But let's be honest. Those of us who have given birth know that growing a baby inside your body and then squirting it out isn't a picnic. There's a lot of pain and suffering. But what results is not only a phenomenal event, but also God's gift. He has also given us other gifts that, through accepting them, require discomfort and suffering. Here, too, the consummation is delightful, and if you've ever enjoyed a meal, you, too have basked in the glory.

APRIL 1989, HOEDSPRUIT, SOUTH AFRICA

I couldn't help but notice the extreme conditions in which some of the African natives live. While some South Africans have many of the luxuries that we have, like televisions and cars, some live without basic necessities like running water. It's amazing to see how different a culture can be from one ecosystem to another. It made my problems seem petty. Curious about what the natives thought of us foreigners who come with expensive jewelry and cameras, I asked our host in Hoedspruit to tell me how he thought they really felt. Undoubtedly, I was told, those people who put dirt in bathtubs and slept in them thought Americans were wasteful and looked at us as an unhappy society because we need so many things. What we see as a destitute situation—a family that makes its home out of cardboard boxes, brush, and debris and lives on fifteen dollars or less a month—is really quite the opposite. Many African natives live off the land and are incredibly spiritual. They feel that they have been given exactly what they need to survive. And somehow, they do. We were always greeted with a smile from our African friends. Sometimes you can't even find that in your own hometown, or from your neighbor. Sure, there are incredibly impoverished and chillingly atrocious conditions in Africa, along with the AIDS epidemic, but is there something simple we can learn from these people?

On every trip to Africa I return feeling as though the experience has changed my life. I want to live more quietly, basically, and spiritually. I appreciate the amenities I have so much more than I did before. I look at people and situations differently—as opportunities to make soulful connections. I look at nature and wildlife as God's gift to us; to feed us and clothe us, and to respect its beauty.

The African natives are surprised that we don't see nature as a healer, the way they do. Like a dog that eats grass when it's sick, an African will know exactly what plant or tree bark can cure an ailment. They have everything they need at their fingertips. They go to sleep with smiles on their faces, not knowing the real meaning of stress. Sometimes I want that.

CHAPTER FIVE

Wang Dang Sweet Poontang—Groupies

Avarice, ambition, lust, etc. are nothing but a species of madness.

—Benedict [Baruch] Spinoza

The first time I saw my husband on stage, I'll admit, I thought he was wildly sexy, fabulously talented, and I felt blessed beyond belief that he'd chosen me to be his wife. With his guitar still strapped around his neck and snug up against his bare chest, Ted ran across the stage with the power of a charging buffalo and then, seemingly effortlessly, he lunged with his long, lean, powerful legs into the most seductive stance, as if some famous choreographer had spent months deciding exactly what would make him look the best. It was mesmerizing, and quite impressive to say the least, especially since he never missed a guitar lick. In twenty-six years I had never seen anything like it before—never having the desire for rock-n-roll music or really being intrigued enough to care. When I saw my husband's first concert, however, what went through my mind was, *Now there's a real man.* Other women, I soon discovered, were thinking the same thing.

Surprisingly, I never saw any groupies at the one and only concert of his that I attended before our wedding. He just kept telling me, "It's over. I'm not interested in anyone else but you, Shemane." Other than have my husband take a polygraph, there was little I could do to test his honesty and love for me. It probably wouldn't have mattered much if there were any groupies backstage during that dreamy period in our relationship anyway. When Ted looked into my eyes, my whole body ached for his flesh and his for mine. We were joined at the hip. Even when he came offstage from his encore, I was there waiting for him with a towel and a cold bottle of water. Each moment we were apart was painful. Love inspires some crazy things, doesn't it? Wars have been fought over the love of a woman. Men have died over what Ted likes to call "twang."

From the moment our eyes met, Ted and I had an undeniable chemistry and bond. Ted was witty and fascinating. When he spoke, he spoke with his entire body. While telling stories, he was descriptive, intelligent, and captivating. He was intense. He was gregarious.

Unlike many men I knew, Ted didn't drink or smoke, and as a fitness enthusiast, neither did I. Ted loved the outdoors and constantly told exciting stories about his worldly travels. He was comfortable with himself, never trying to mislead anyone about who he really was. He was a doting and caring father, and all of those qualities were exactly what I was looking for in a man. My man just happened to perform on stage in front of thousands of people.

I hadn't been to many concerts as a teenager, so I had little to which I could relate the concert-going experience. Sports, student council, and boys had held my interest. I was too busy going to cheerleading, swimming, or gymnastics practice to go to concerts. Had I known about the flagrant women who swarmed the rock-n-roll scene, I would have set some boundaries with Ted. Some major-league rock-n-roll wives put a stop to their husband's backstage meet-and-greets, where radio contest winners and other hangers-on meet the band. Historically, this has often been the place where the band members pick out their cavorting partners for an after-show rendezvous, sometimes even before the show!

It wasn't until after we were married that groupies came out of the woodwork. It was amazing to me that even in my presence, girls exposed her bare chest, with Rocco and me sitting right next to Ted. I cannot believe the audacity of some people. I was absolutely appalled. (Now might be a good time to talk to your teenage daughters about what they do at concerts, moms and dads.) Thankfully, Ted told her to cover herself and then he signed her shirt. Did she think that Ted would just dive right in, when his wife and newborn baby were sitting next to him? People are weird.

The largest silent pestilence on society, I believe, is women who chase married men. When marriages and families are broken, it's the children who suffer most. Mothers, please expose this truth to your daughters. A woman who makes the choice to sleep with a married man possesses a huge lack of morals, character, and good judgment. It destroys innocent families.

Ted made a commitment and promised me he'd never cheat and I was certain he wouldn't. Loose women at his concerts, he always said, never meant anything to him. AIDS and many other sexually transmitted diseases were so prevalent. Why would *anyone* jeopardize his or her life for sex? Ted and I had a very good relationship. We had a family to raise. He couldn't consider risking all of that for a little floozy, could he?

Reality set in quickly. Shortly after we were married Ted went on a successful tour with Tommy Shaw, Jack Blades, and Michael Cartellone of the Damn Yankees. They toured for the better part of eighteen months, and my imagination ran rampant. The more I learned about the music industry, the more I became jealous. At the Damn Yankees concerts I started seeing more and more groupies, and I started to become more and more worried. Ted had always been flirtatious with other women, but I assumed much of his cavorting would cease after he had found me, his soul mate.

After the first month of our marriage, his old "female friends" were still telephoning our house. When one of them phoned at 4 A.M. "just to talk," I finally got fed up, and told Ted I wanted the calls to stop.

Ted agreed, and the phone calls stopped immediately.

Because Ted is an entertainer, and especially because he's in the rock-n-roll business, it's often assumed that he'll flirt with any woman who's within an earshot. It goes with the territory. Unfortunately, he did well living up to that assumption. The level to which he sank, however, was demeaning—for me, anyway. For him, and every other red-blooded American male, he was living the American Dream, with half-naked women coming out of the woodwork, the staircase, the closet, or wherever they could with their phone numbers practically written on their foreheads, ready to "go at it" right then and there if Ted said it was okay. For me, as his wife, I was embarrassed by this blatant display of sexuality, and I became even more jealous as Ted left for more tours and I was left at home.

Once when I was at home nursing our son, I turned on the television, excited to watch my husband on a national TV interview, but then nearly had a heart attack when the camera pulled back to show that another woman was sitting on his lap, fondling his hair. A different heartbreaking time was a phone call I received from another Damn Yankees wife who informed me that one of Ted's old girlfriends was following him on the road from concert to concert, even traveling on the bus. Of course, my husband wholeheartedly denied any wrongdoing and alleged that any girls he saw were just friends. Desperately, I wanted to believe him and I wished that I didn't care, but the truth was that I did. Seeing him flirt with other women made me physically ill. When someone with whom you're intimate makes sexual remarks to other women, it bruises your soul. Some women, ice-cold and hardened women, say that when their spouse flirts it doesn't bother them. I say they're lying.

LITTLE MISS DANGEROUS

I am aware of several situations in which a groupie has latched on to a musician purely for the fame and fortune of being married to a rock star, convincing herself and him that their union would work. This is dangerous and, in fact, exactly what complicates and eventually dissolves many celebrity marriages. There is something about the rock-n-roll industry that causes people to completely abandon logic. They get caught up in the lights and paparazzi and think that for some strange reason all of it is meaningful, when in truth they're really searching for something more.

We all desperately need love and attention. Groupies, I believe, just didn't get enough of it as children. Certainly all of us women want to look our best, and we'll go through a hell of a lot to do it, dyeing our hair, plucking our eyebrows, ardently exercising to stay in shape. When we compromise our integrity to call attention to ourselves by dressing indecently, or in a way that would make our grandmothers embarrassed, however, we've crossed the line. Don't worry; I'm not impervious to this superficiality. There was a time, early on in our marriage, when I was green and inexperienced and didn't know how to say what I wanted and my husband wasn't exactly pushing away the lovely young women who threw themselves at him day and night. I was so determined to find a way to keep his interest, I succumbed to the nonsensical notion of breast augmentation. Now, of course, I wish I hadn't. The reason I'm sharing this with the world is because it's all so trivial. Implants don't matter. Hair dye doesn't matter. Eyebrows don't matter. Pink nail polish versus a French manicure doesn't really matter in the long run. What matters is heart and soul. What matters most is the love you share with someone. Throughout my marriage to Ted, I've learned the true meaning of marriage vows, especially the part that says, *For better or worse, in sickness and in health.* That is what's important in life.

Now that I've survived my twenties and thirties and have successfully entered my forties, I can look back on all the silly things I've done and see that my hair color or the clothes I wear are not really indicative of who I am inside. If all of that were taken away, or if I was in an accident like Christopher Reeve, in what way would any of that superficial nonsense make a difference? I'll bet Christopher Reeve would rather hug his son than have the most awesome hair weave any day. Fortunately, through our TNUSA organization, my feet are put back on the ground when I have the blessed opportunity to meet and stay in touch with fantastic people like our friend Chip Stewart, who never let something like a debilitating illness determine his quality of life. Another young friend of ours, Zac Martin, went hunting with Ted last year. You'd never know it by looking at him, because his bright smile always got in the way, but Zac had bone cancer. His mother, Tammy, was just as bright and bubbly as her six-foot, four-inch-tall son, and I found myself wondering if I'd be that way, too, if my son had terminal cancer. I imagined that they were just happy to be there with us, hunting, which was one of Zac's last wishes. Sadly, at only sixteen short years of age, Zac passed away and will be very strongly missed, but I can tell you that he has made a huge difference in our world.

My life with Ted is one of drastic dichotomies, but it only makes me appreciate every opportunity I have not only to make the world a better place, but continue to improve the qualities in myself that might need a little upgrade, as well. I am saddened, however, for these young girls who throw themselves at rock stars and their crew members, because these days the disappointment can be more than just an unreturned phone call. A one-night stand with a rock star could result in a sexually transmitted disease or, worse, an unwanted pregnancy. It happens often, unfortunately, even these days. Obviously, not all rock-n-roll musicians are philanderers, but it does go with the territory and it is hard to deny the sexual allure when the band is traveling on the road

Chapter Six

This Side of Hell

Once you know the truth, you cannot go back to not knowing. Living the truth that you know is the greatest service you can offer the world.

—Iyanla Vanzant

IT WAS ON THAT BRILLIANTLY BRIGHT SEPTEMBER AFTERNOON in Nashville at the celebrity shoot that I began to realize that I was in a quandary. Certainly I was thrilled to be there watching my husband participate in the Louise Mandrell Celebrity Shoot. Sitting proudly on a picnic table watching him perform, however, had me relaxed and nervous at the same time. Were Ted's dark sunglasses hiding something? He had seemed unusually calm that day, to the point that my instincts picked up a "red alert." All summer, during his tour, Ted had been extraordinarily agitated by the smallest detail gone awry. Something was wrong. I knew it. I just didn't know what. Or maybe I didn't really want to know.

Even after so many married years together I still adored my husband. Watching his handsome face and his long lean legs made me want to hug him and tell him that whatever it was that was bothering him, we could get through it as one. Ted did look drawn and distressed, and I was surprised that he was missing so many shots. It appeared as if he didn't even care, and that was a startling, out-of-character sign.

We were scheduled to leave our deluxe Nashville hotel suite the next day, so we relaxed that evening and spent the next morning in bed. I couldn't have been more content. We ordered fresh strawberries, croissants, and coffee and snuggled in our plush white hotel robes. CNN was on the television and Ted flipped the channels several times, as usual, but then did something different. He turned the television off, paused, took a deep breath, and then turned it back on again. It seemed as though he was about to say something, but then he became uncomfortably quiet. I wanted to ask him what was on his mind, but I didn't. As we lay side by side, he brushed the hair from my face and held me close. I was so happy. I thought about the day we first met and how far we had come. Moments later, he did it again. Abruptly, he turned the television off once more, but this time he got out of bed, leaned over, and scooped me up in his arms. Our suite had an adjoining living room and Ted carried me to a chair next to a window.

"What are you doing?" I asked, wondering if he was just being romantic. Saying nothing, he lowered me gently into the cushy chair, and knelt down in front of me. Then he dropped his head on my knees and buried his face in my robe. His body began to shake. "What's wrong?" I asked, feeling an ominous, overwhelming emotion that something terrible had happened. My initial concern was that he was seriously ill and hadn't told me. After all, he was a man in his late forties taking on the workload of several men. Maybe it was time for the Motor City Madman to slow down.

I thought it couldn't happen to me, to us, but between sobs he told me that he had "made a terrible mistake," and from that point on I knew what he was implying.

"Two years ago," he said while hugging me tightly, "I had an affair."

My heart stopped. I gasped! This wasn't really happening to me, was it? Although I heard him loud and clear, the dimensions of the mistake had not yet sunk in. Looking out the window, watching nothing in particular, I was wondering if this was all just a dream. And at that moment I realized that I died. I know I did. I couldn't hear, see, or smell. It was a brief period of nothingness. An abysmal emptiness took over. There was nothing, no sound, no emotion, no tears, no warmth or cold. Nothing. I was dead. My life, as I had known it, would never be the same.

Ted was totally remorseful and begged me for forgiveness. He wanted to remain in the marriage and work this out, whatever it took. The brief affair stopped before it started. So that wasn't the problem. The weight of this secret had been too much for him. We had been too close for too long, and keeping this from me just felt wrong to him. We had been more than just lovers and friends, husband and wife. We were soul mates, and living with this secret was causing him restless nights and ill health. We'd made a promise when we got married to never keep secrets from each other, and he knew that this affair was exactly what that meant.

Somehow, I had to be certain that he'd never, ever repeat the same mistake. How could I know? How could I ever trust him again? I thought of Mick Jagger's former wife, model Jerry Hall, and so many other celebrities who have reportedly tolerated their husbands' affairs. Hillary Clinton, Michael Jordan's wife, Halle Berry. Good grief. *Halle Berry?* How could you do any better than that?

My whole world instantly became shattered glass. Tiny slivers of sparkling prisms scattered everywhere. My mind was filled with rage, anger, sadness, and yet it was stagnant. I was in shock. It was several tormenting moments before tears began to pour out of my eyes. My body just shut down. Breathing was difficult. Standing, or sitting, too. I was lost. My arms and legs shook uncontrollably. My breathing quickened, as if I couldn't get enough air. It seemed as though all of the life force had just been sucked from my body. Had I been shot, mugged, or assaulted, the result would have been the same.

Gone were the images of a carefree family, trusting and safe. A happy family. Loving. Secure. Trusting. Gone. We would never have faithfulness in our marriage again, and that was tormenting. The quality of my being, my existence, would be traumatically altered forever. *Forever. Till death do us part.* What happened to the vows we took? So this is what the *for better and for worse* part meant. Now I was certain that my jealous concerns about the rock-n-roll groupies had been substantiated. My worst nightmare had come true.

Still, I knew that nothing I could have done, short of being there, would have stopped Ted from committing adultery. Opportunity knocked, a groupie was there, and I wasn't. I also had to be thankful that he'd decided to tell me when he didn't have to. But, really, how could I do that?

It dawned on me that we had to get dressed and catch a plane. I had a life waiting for me. I had to move on, but I couldn't. A strange, overwhelming feeling of detachment prevailed. I didn't even care if I got on a plane to go home. Nothing seemed to matter. I didn't know what to do, or how to function. I felt like I was walking dead. How could I suddenly turn back into the doting mother I had always been? How could I smile and pretend to the world that nothing was wrong?

Instantly, I was bitter that my fairy-tale romance had been taken from me. We had something so wonderful. We were soul mates. The connection we had could only be compared to the ones trashy novels describe. We were inseparable. But then our marriage, our beautiful painting, a one-of-a-kind masterpiece, was destroyed in a few thoughtless moments.

A painter sits above the beach on a hilltop overlooking the ocean. He blissfully dabs his cerulean-tipped paintbrush on the canvas and creates a magnificent blue, cloudless sky. M-shaped seagulls and a gleaming sun add dimension to the scene. Milky white and salmon-colored seashells cover the beach, just above the waterline. The painter's masterpiece is nearly complete. He sits back in his chair and examines his work. He is satisfied. And then an onlooker heaves a can of black paint all over the canvas. The paint splatters in the middle of the painting and drips down the easel to the ground. Immediately, the bewildered artist tries to wipe off the mutilated canvas.

Why would someone do such a thing? he wonders. Although most of the thick paint can be removed, the masterpiece is ruined. A horrible dark stain is left on the canvas. While wiping, the painter erases the seagulls and the sun. The shells are no longer light pink, but an ugly dark green. People come by to see the painter's work and are appalled. They cover their mouths with their hands to hide their shocked expressions. The painter quickly tries to camouflage the black-stained canvas with white paint. The once beautiful, unpolluted painting is now marred with a gray cast. It will never be the same. The seashells are broken.

After Ted told me he had an affair, I knew the stain on the canvas would always be there. We would never have fidelity in our marriage. My cherished family painting was severely damaged, if not destroyed. I was in a deep stage of denial, and then it dawned on me. This explained his recent erratic behavior during the summer tour. All along, he really did have something on his mind. Even more, I was saddened with the thought that he'd borne this burden for so long without me.

Because we had always been inseparable, I realized that Rocco would know if something had upset me. He was, and is, a very sensitive and caring young boy. It would be extremely difficult to hide my emotions from him. We were buddies. I knew it would be a battle to go from bawling my eyes out to "What would you like for lunch, honey?" I had to become an actress, quickly.

Everything was surreal, like I was riding slow motion in a car and people were saying something to me, but I couldn't understand what it was.

When we arrived at our house I looked at it like it was the first time I had seen it. Something had changed drastically since I'd left, and yet nothing had. Our dogs were happy to see us, as usual. They bolted out of the kennels and ran circles around us. I wanted to smile but I couldn't. The muscles in my face were frozen. My heart, I thought, had been ripped out of my chest, thrown against the wall, and splattered.

Knowing that other men and women endure this same traumatic experience was somewhat consoling. I was not alone. Adultery has no boundaries, race, or creed; it's happened among royalty and poverty, in every nation, since the dawn of time. During this same time, plastered on the front covers of magazines were pictures of princes and presidents who'd committed adultery during their marriages.

A multitude of feelings surged through me. Should I stay married and work things out, or get a divorce and raise a son on my own? To live without Ted was something I didn't want to do, but somehow I felt that others would look down on me if I endured and condoned his affair. Would staying with the (unfaithful) man I loved send messages to people that I let Ted take advantage of me, or that I was strong?

My heart ached more than it ever had in my life. There were times when it actually felt as though I was driving myself insane with my own questions. How could I go on? Then I would think about the obvious warning signs of Ted's affair: his irritable demeanor, complaints of slight physical illness, and escalating agitated behavior. How could I have missed them?

Each one of us has our own personal nightmare, whether it's losing a job, mounting bills, cancer, or losing a loved one. Someone who has experienced the rolling waves in the high seas, I began to rationalize, would recognize the pain better than a therapist who has read a book and passed a test. This book, although filled with rock-n-roll Nuge history, would also be a way for me to comfort someone else who might have been betrayed, and also serve as a way to show my healing journey. We have all endured situations that threatened

about sharing my private thoughts with the world. Some might wonder why I would want to expose this tumultuous interval in my life for the entire world to twist into their own sordid interpretation. Many people, including close friends and relatives, have questioned my desire to reveal such an unchaste and personal event. Some might wonder why I would choose to put my family through even more anguish and unwanted publicity by writing this book. For more than four years now, I have struggled with that very question. Morning, noon, and night, I have often wondered why this particular event happened to me. What did I do to deserve such betrayal from someone I loved so deeply and who I thought loved me as well? What kind of a test was God giving me? What could I possibly learn from this?

It's hard to believe I can even say this, but suffering helped me to gain a greater understanding of life. Through hatred and sorrow and grief and pity I found a kinder, gentler path of living. I learned compassion and forgiveness. By changing my thought process, I discovered, I could transform my restlessness, my anger, my heartache into peace! Simply altering the way in which I viewed my husband's affair helped me to see that it was an opportunity for me to change, as well.

Married to a Rock Star initially evolved as a way for me to tell my story about the hardship of life on the road, the myriad business dealings, and abundance of sluts—I mean groupies. But something was missing. A little voice in the back of my mind kept urging me to be honest and disclose the myth. Writing this book became a responsibility and a covenant I had with God. It was gratifying during extreme times when it was difficult to find joy in anything. Writing became therapeutic, insightful, and rehabilitative. It was a way of turning my personal tragedy into something creative and enlightening. I felt that in sharing our hardship with the world, I might somehow turn a negative situation into something positive.

It was, in fact, because of my love for Ted that I wrote this book. We continue the challenging, yet rewarding process of making our marriage work. We are successfully mending the torn pieces of our relationship. And I must say, I am ever so grateful that we did. We are much happier now than we've ever been. Every moment is an amazing opportunity to renew our love for each other. We acknowledge what happened, learn from it, and move on.

Sharing what I've learned with people who have been unwillingly thrown into the dark muddle of despair and emptiness, as I have, is a way for me to turn the tables. It is an opportunity for me to take a negative experience and turn it into something positive. Sharing this information has helped me heal. And if I can help someone survive an infidelity, or if I can prevent someone—even one person—from committing adultery, then I will have made a difference in another person's life. That is why I have written this book.

If I can stop the beautiful woven tapestry of one family from being ripped apart at the seams, as mine almost has been, if I can help one man or woman cope with the same trauma I've endured, if I can save a child from being separated from one parent in a nasty divorce, then my tragedy has had a positive effect. That is why I have written this book and why I have shared my story with you. If I can convince at least one person that entering into an improper relationship isn't worth the risk, then, somehow, to someone, my devastation can have meaning. *For God's sake, don't do it!*

STATE OF SHOCK

William F. Mitchell, author of *Adultery: Facing its Reality,* has spent decades accumulating startling statistics about infidelity and how it affects not only the involved parties, but also their families, as well.

- 10–20% of cheating begins as Internet affairs in chat rooms
- 75% of adulterers are middle-class wage earners
- 60–70% of adultery victims are women

- 10–20% of adultery victims claim to be Christians and attend regular church activities
- 99.9% deny they are having an affair
- 10–25% of spouses having affairs bring financial ruin to their marital home
- 100% of extramarital affairs take their toll on biological and stepchildren
- 10–15% of marriages survive affairs after counseling.

Chances are that you or someone you know has been involved in or affected by an affair. It's not just happening in the entertainment industry. Cheaters come from all walks of life and from almost everywhere. The case of Clara Harris, an enraged Texas wife who ran over her husband, killing him, after having been confronted by his mistress, makes us aware of just what a *woman scorned* can do.

Unfortunately, infidelity just happens way too often. Maggie Scarf, author of the book *Intimate Partners,* suggests that as many as 65 percent of men and 55 percent of women cheat. We are devaluing the very entity that holds us all together and that created us: the love between a man and a woman. For most of us, that's why we're here. The sacred covenant we call marriage is taken all too lightly these days. It's a shame, really, when you think of the months, sometimes even years people spend planning elaborate weddings with tens of thousands of dollars doled out by loving parents who work hard for that cash reserve and think *This is it* for their son or daughter, only to discover that their son ran off with his secretary or their daughter had a fling with the pool boy. The children must be separated and swapped like an assembly line, moving their precious belongs from Daddy's house to Mommy's house because Daddy and Mommy made poor choices. So let's go back to the chalkboard. Who really suffers?

The children.

Is it a coincidence that as we've devalued the institution of marriage and the family so casually over the past fifty years, school SAT scores have dropped and there are approximately fifteen million new cases of sexually transmitted diseases and nearly one million teenage girls who get pregnant every year? (This is according to the Centers for Disease Control.) It seems as though, as a society, we've been reluctant to acknowledge the suggestion that two parents are better than one because it might hurt someone's feelings. *Tough.* If you made the decision to have children—that is, had sex—you had better be prepared for a lifetime of even more difficult choices, because guess what? God's intended result for lovemaking is the miracle of a baby!

We should place more emphasis and value on raising children and keeping the family unit intact. The recent increase in violent crimes has even been linked to lack of a father figure in the house.

- Boys raised outside intact marriages are, on average, more than twice as likely as other boys to wind up in jail—with each year spent without a dad increasing the odds of future incarceration by 5 percent.
- A child born to an unwed mother is about 2.5 times more likely to end up in prison, while one whose parents split during his teen years was about 1.5 times more likely to be imprisoned.
- Boys living in stepparent families were almost three times as likely to face incarceration.
- While living in poverty made it more likely a boy would go to jail, family structure was more important than income. (National Center for Policy Analysis)
- Teenage boys living with just their single fathers were no more likely to commit crimes than boys coming from intact families. But boys living with remarried fathers faced rates of future incarceration as high as or higher than boys living with remarried mothers. *(Wall Street Journal)*

and spiritually, all of America suffers and takes on the burden when bad choices are made.

We hire men and women to teach our children how to read and write and spell—and now do just about everything else with a computer. I'm uncomfortable with the idea of having a stranger teaching an unknown human sexuality curriculum to my child. Who's in charge of choosing that particular agenda? It varies from school to school and, quite frankly, that's wrong. As parents, it's *our responsibility* to teach our kids about safe sex or, preferably, abstinence. Fifty years ago our grandparents would have been appalled if they heard some of the things that go on in schools today, especially when public schools have the authority to hand out condoms. What goes on between two people, whether gay or straight, is best left behind closed doors, and shouldn't be taught, I believe to young, naive girls and boys. With same-sex marriages becoming more accepted, does that mean that eventually our public school systems will be pressured into teaching our kids how same-sex couples have sex? What about the guy down the street who's into bestiality? Eventually he's going to want to have his voice heard.

Even with the best government-paid programs, however, we cannot be certain the message hits home. Teaching family planning and sex education to teenagers can have a boomerang effect, as Dr. Jacqueline Kasun discovered:

> I found that adolescent pregnancy has increased in the United States since the introduction of the government sex programs in Humboldt County, where we have several "model" programs and government family planning expenditures per person have been much higher than in the nation, adolescent pregnancy has increased ten times as much as in the nation. The reason this increase in pregnancy has not resulted in an increase in births is that Humboldt County has had a greater than one-thousand percent increase in teenage abortions during the

> past decade. This increase is more than fifteen times as high as the increase for the nation. The evidence clearly indicates that government family planning-sex education programs aggravate the problems they seek to correct.

We have all but forgotten the very idea of why we have sex in the first place. It should not be hurtful or destructive to a third party, or end in killing a fetus. It should be a sacred, spiritual, private activity between two loving, consenting, and married adults. (It's just so much easier that way.)

In order to drive on the highway, you must take a course that requires at least some reading and studying, and you must also spend hours demonstrating your ability to perform these tasks in front of another, more experienced driver. Then, and only then, are you allowed to take a test, wait for the results, and finally be allowed the privilege to drive. A license to marry, on the other hand, can be obtained in a fraction of the time in Las Vegas. All that's required is a witness, who can be acquired for a small fee, and of course a person to perform the ceremony, like a justice of the peace—Elvis-style, if you like—for a nominal charge, as well. In less than the time it takes to get a couple of flapjacks, you can also get hitched to the person of your dreams, or to whomever you just spent the night with.

Eventually fornication en masse will only lead to a society full of soulless, spiritually bankrupt individuals who are in continual search for something that's never to be found, much like the attention groupies so desperately seek. I know of one woman who got backstage, met the boys in the band (not Ted's), and was invited to travel with them for two weeks. The unfortunate truth was that she left behind a young daughter and a husband who, as you could probably guess, were appalled by her sudden and blatant abandonment of morals and convictions. Her husband divorced her and won custody of their daughter. In a haphazard instant, she threw her life away. *For*

Nugent
FAMILY ALBUM

Mr. & Mrs. Whackmaster.

Rockin' in 2000.

The Nuge and
Sonny Crockett
(Don Johnson).
—1986

The big wedding celebration, January 21, 1989.

Sealed with a kiss.

Rocco's smile lit up the room (1990).

Ted reporting at the 1992 Republican Convention for MTV in Nashville.

Rocco says his dad is crazy...

...but he plays a mean guitar, Mom!

Shemane and her Tommy.

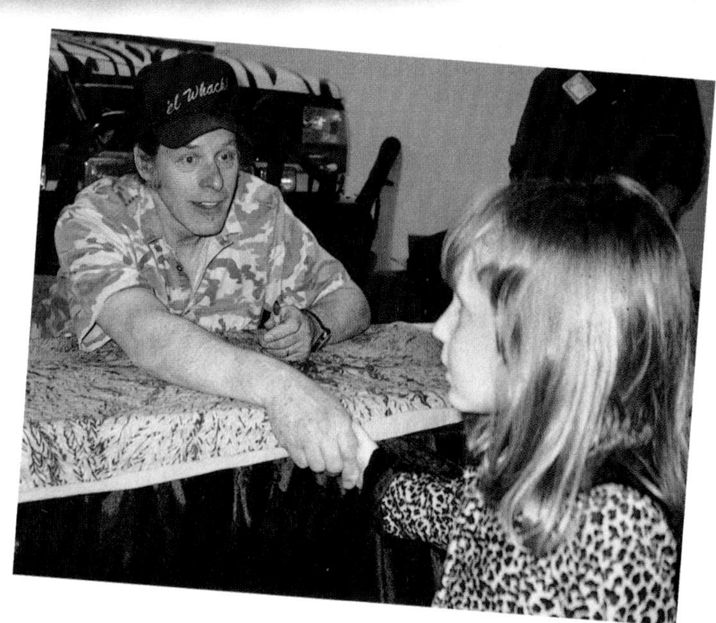

Ted at a 'meet & greet.'

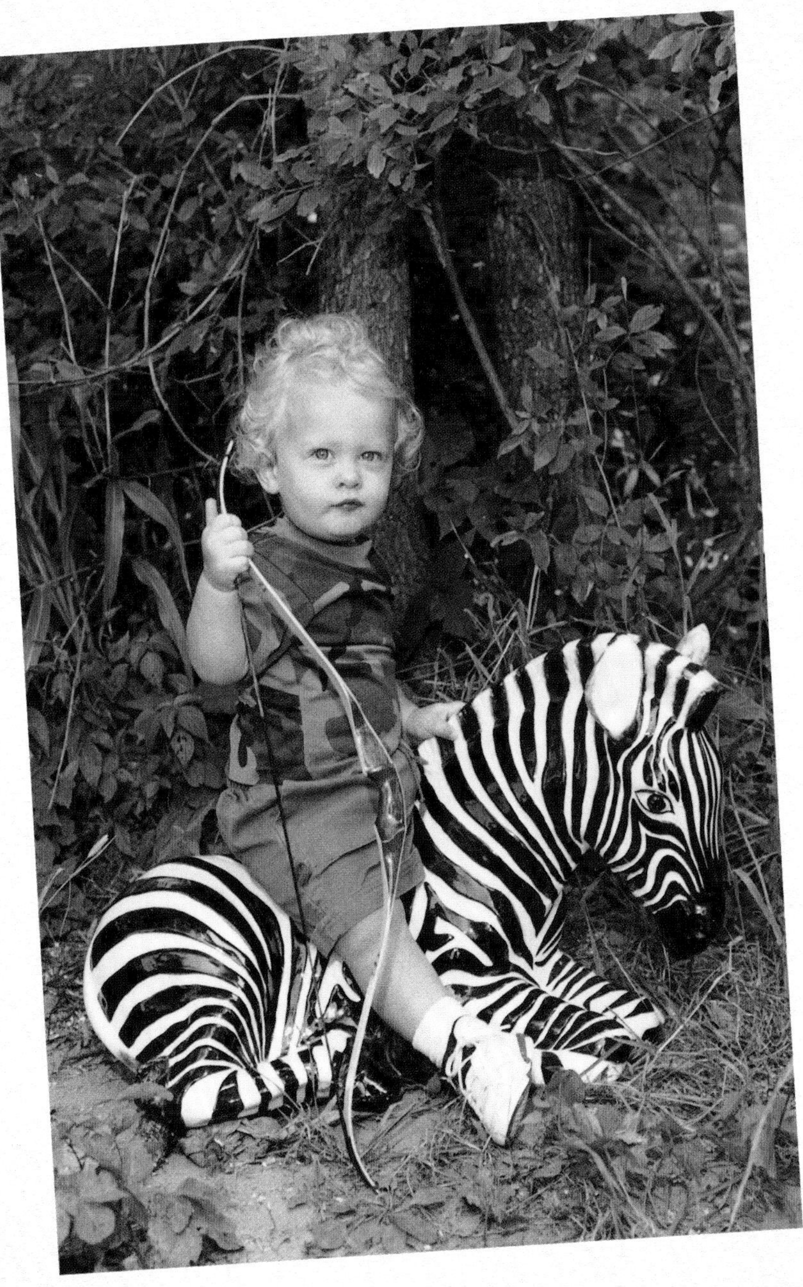

Credit: Hal Folk

Rocco's first bow (and zebra ride, too!)

Family squg.

The early days, when Shemane raced four-wheelers.

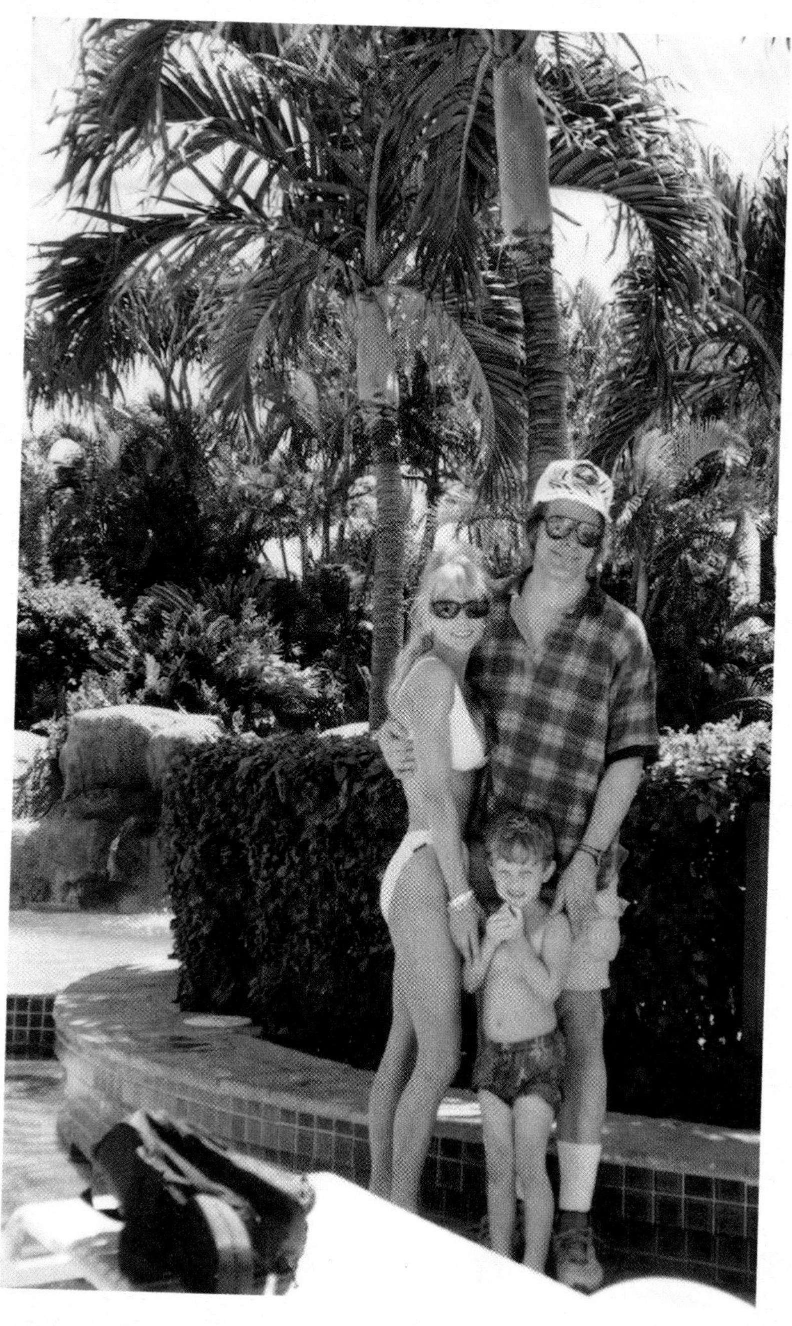

Hawaii is the dream vacation destination, as Ted can go hunting while Rocco and Shemane can play at the pool.

Archery as discipline.

Ted, Rocco, and Gonzo the Wonder Lab.

Shemane, Rocco, Toby, Ted, and Sasha pose for photos for the Ted Nugent Adventure Outdoors Magazine.

Joe Perry, Steven Tyler, Kid Rock, Ted, Shemane, Rocco, and Linda Peterson.

Rocco, Shemane, Ted, Elmore Leonard, Joe and Billie Perry and friend, backstage at an Aerosmith concert in Detroit.

Linda Peterson, Kid Rock, Ted, Shemane, and Rocco just before Ted and Kid Rock go onstage to jam with Aerosmith.

The Nugents and e Kennedys at a George Magazine party in New York City.

Ted says he's "Scaring white folks."

Sermon on the mount.

Shemane and members of the Detroit Red Wings backstage at the Palace, at an Aerosmith concert

Backstage after a rockout.

Rocco and Shemane (in darker days) with Vice President Dan Quayle and friends.

Backstage, Ted and Shemane meet up with KISS (Ace Frehley, Paul Stanley, Peter Criss, and Gene Simmons), and Peter Criss's wife Gigi.

Ted's favorite bowhunting buddy is Angela Kline, who visited the Nuge and KISS backstage before a concert.

Shemane and her first white-tailed buck, taken in Texas.

Watch out, Wolfie (Van Halen).

Shemane's first axis buck was a fun family hunt, at the Y.O. Ranch in Texas.

Ted, Shemane, and Rocco hunting in Alaska.

Shemane and her heroes: Ted, Charlton Heston, and Rocco.

Ted and fellow crooners Kid Rock and Bob Seger.

The entire Nugent Clan: Starr, Ted, Riley, Shemane, Sasha, Toby, and Rocco.

Whackmaster Jr. reporting for duty.

Ted served on the council of the Sportsmen for (Michigan's Governor John) Engler. Here, he and longtime hunting friend, former Detroit Tiger Kirk Gibson, wait their turn to talk to the press.

Governor John Engler and wife Michelle at Ted's 50th birthday party.

Rocco at his first Damn Yankees concert.

Shemane and her main squeeze.

Ted and Shemane at the National Association of Music Merchants (N.A.M.M.) show in L.A., waiting to sign autographs.

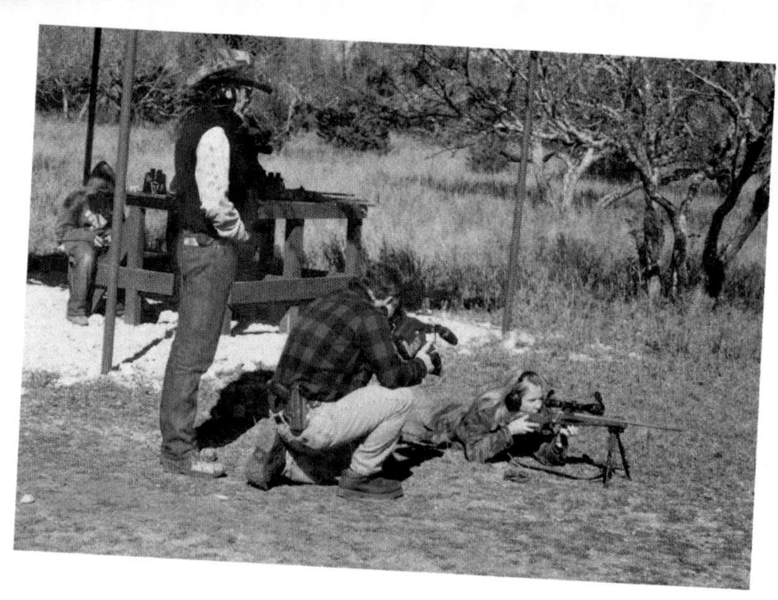

Taping for the Ted Nugent Spirit of the Wild show. That's Jim Lawson behind the camera.

Conan O'Brien, the Nuge, and their favorite toys.

Renewing vows, February 2000.

Tribe Nuge at the vow renewal ceremony.

Rocco and Mom taking a break from skiing in Aspen.

Shemane, Rocco, and their favorite Survivor, Mike Skupin (2002).

Shemane and her custom zebra .22.

Two finalists in the American drool contest.

Rocco's first horseback ride, with Dad supervising.

Onstage, Shemane delivers Ted's guitar, and a little something extra.

what? Unquestionably, she must now feel ashamed of her behavior. She set an appalling example for her daughter and ruined many other lives in the process. Having affairs devalues the significance of the bond between husband and wife, parent and child.

When nearly half of all hospital beds in America are occupied by people with emotional disturbances, I believe that there is a grave need for more discussions such as this. We didn't get married to get divorced, and most other people don't, either, so if my "coming out" can have even the slightest effect on so many of the broken homes and battered children who endure traumatic breakups from their parents' bad decisions, such as infidelity, I have contributed to a deep, spiritual awakening that was necessary.

Life is all about choices, really, and Ted and I are willing to expose this affliction, while risking his reputation, in order to bring to light an issue that is devastating American families and creating confused children and way too many broken homes. We're taking a gamble here because we see the value in mending a marriage for the sake of children, for the vows we once took, and because it's the right thing to do. It worked for us, and there's no question that children would rather have Mommy and Daddy together in a loving relationship than separated or divorced. Undeniably, in extreme cases of physical or verbal abuse or mental disorders associated with one of the spouses, separation and even divorce may be inevitable.

Ted and I are proof that a couple can make a mistake and move on and be very, very happy. Even after fourteen years of marriage, we miss each other every moment that we're apart, and when we are, we call each other incessantly. It would have been easier for me to divorce my husband and collect a check every month. Ultimately, however, I wouldn't have been happy, and I know that the situation would not have been best for all of our kids. Even Ted's adult children crave structure and family rituals like spending holiday celebrations together. One of the nicest compliments I ever received came from my stepdaughter

Sasha when she discovered our dilemma. "Please don't leave us," she said when she heard I might, and gave me a long hug.

Certainly I could have carried on with my life as it was, never mentioning a word to another soul about this deep dark secret we hid in the closet like Pandora's box, always aware of its presence but hoping it would just go away; afraid that if we ever opened it up Medusa's head would pop out. While nothing can ever make the weight of this secret and its ugliness disappear, I recognized the value in my potential contribution. Is my purpose in life to crawl under a rock and hide? I think not. As painful as this is for me, for Ted, and for our family, I still believe that speaking out about this predicament is the right thing to do, because to prevent what I know to be a devastating life event for someone else has brought me comfort, healing, and peace.

There certainly aren't many people in the rock-n-roll world willing to discuss their religious convictions, but I am and Ted is, and our faith is what carried us through our darkest hour. On February 10, 2001, we renewed our marriage vows to cement the ties that bind us in front of God, our family, and close friends. We are more in love than we have ever been, happy that we persevered for us and our family, and elated that we paused to remember why we got married in the first place.

More and more, I'm pleased to find that once in a while I come across people in the entertainment industry who are open to the topic of spirituality; on occasion backstage discussions can get surprisingly introspective, or even break into prayer. When the WWJD bracelet craze was going on several years ago, I always had a stash of them in case I could give one away to a newly converted Christian or one of Rocco's friends. Once, when Steven Tyler and Joe Perry had come to our house to do a little handgun training and shooting with Ted, Steven asked about all the bracelets on Rocco's and my wrists (we often wore two or three at a time). We translated the acronym "What Would Jesus Do" to Steven, and he told us about how his first singing gig was actually in church. Rocco smiled. Stepping out of my comfort zone a bit, I noticed that Steven usually wore a lot of bracelets on his wrists and I offered him one, curious to see what his response would be. "Yeah," he said. "I'd wear one." That night onstage, in front of twenty thousand screaming fans, Steven Tyler wore the WWJD bracelet I gave him. For the first time, I thought that maybe I could make a difference even in this crazy rock-n-roll world in which I surprisingly found myself. There I was, spreading the Christian message to Aerosmith's Steven Tyler. And why not?

Inevitably, I will receive an onslaught of criticism for airing my dirty laundry. Persecution, I believe, has come to those much braver than myself. My husband, quite frankly, has the most to lose in all of this and has suffered just as much as I have. It wasn't exactly easy for Ted to endure my taunting after he told me about his affair. It might have been easier for him, too, to have just given up the struggle and allowed our relationship to die, just as so many other couples do. Fortunately, he realized the mistake he made could have cost him the most important thing in his life: his family.

Ted taught me to be proactive, and this book is my attempt to bring awareness of a destructive blight in America that desperately needs change. My prayers, you see, have been answered here, because although I will never forget the pain Ted and I endured, I can empathize with others who endure not just similar tribulations, but *any tribulation,* and share my thoughts and insights with them, helping them ease their pain. Through teaching, I've learned, comes compassion, patience, and healing. As stated in a phenomenal book called *A Course in Miracles,* "Whenever you offer a miracle to another, you are shortening the suffering of both of you."

The opportunity I have had to make a difference in the lives of others, through my Queen of the Forest programs, teaching hundreds of fitness classes, as a parent, or through opening my heart and soul in this book is very significant to me. Yes, I'm taking a risk here—it's a choice I've made—but as author Sarah Ban Breathnach believes, "Many of us don't think of choice as a spiritual gift. We believe choices are burdens to be endured, not embraced. And so they become burdens." It's true that I once allowed the situation I was in to become burdensome (and at times still do), but Ban Breathnach also suggests that "there are only three ways to change the trajectory of our lives for better or worse: crisis, chance, and choice." And that's exactly what I'm doing here: taking a chance by exposing my hardships, in the hopes of helping others, but dealing with my crisis at the same time.

No, my husband isn't perfect. Neither am I and neither are you, so don't go squawking about how the Motor City Madman couldn't handle the pressure. Nearly 70 percent of married men may have already forsaken their marriage vows. Now throw in thousands of beautiful, barely dressed women heaving themselves at you night after night with no watchdog in sight. Any hot-blooded American married man would have a tough time with the *Just say no* modus operandi. As I've stated before, we rock wives realize that if we're not on the road, eventually the groupies could get to even the most married of men. I'm not making excuses for my husband. Even the producers at VH1 recognized it.

Chapter Seven

Damn Yankees

HERE IS THE ANSWER TO YOUR SEARCH FOR PEACE. Here is the key to meaning in a world that seems to make no sense. Here is the way to safety in apparent dangers that appear to threaten you at every turn, and bring uncertainty to all your hopes of ever finding quietness and peace. Here are all questions answered; here the end of all uncertainty ensured at last.

The unforgiving mind is full of fear, and offers love no room to be itself; no place where it can spread its wings in peace and soar above the turmoil of the world. The unforgiving mind is sad, without the hope of respite and release from pain. It suffers and abides in misery, peering about in darkness, seeing not, yet certain of the danger lurking there.

The unforgiving mind is torn with doubt, confused about itself and all it sees; afraid and angry, weak and blustering, afraid to go ahead, afraid to stay, afraid to waken or to go to sleep, afraid of every sound, yet more afraid of stillness; terrified of darkness, yet more terrified at the approach of light.

—*A Course in Miracles,* Lesson 121

Although my life for the past fourteen years has been all about surviving this wondrous rock-n-roll life, the saber-witted producers at VH1 were searching for yet another new and exciting program to corner the ratings market, so they contacted the Motor City Madman to mull over an idea. They wanted to put television cameras all over our house, follow Ted's every move, and put half a dozen city kids together to try to follow Ted doing chores on our SwampHellZone of southern Michigan. It would be like a merger of those two proven television programs, *Survivor* and *The Osbournes. Surviving Nugent* was to be a half-hour comedy–reality pilot that would be raw and compelling. It would take people from different socioeconomic backgrounds, varying ages, all corners of the United States and make them guests at our humble home grounds in rural Michigan. The goal is simple . . . survive the Nuge. Each week would be a wild journey to observe the contestants as they tried to keep up with the Motor City Madman by staying in touch with nature, feeling the dirt beneath their feet and in their hands, and trudging through the swamps with Uncle Ted, stopping only to plant trees along the way.

At the time Rocco and I were commuting from our Florida home, where Rocco was attending a prep school. We flew back to Michigan every other weekend and met Ted on the road wherever he was. VH1 flew us home early one week—getting Rocco out of school—saying that they really wanted us to be involved in the show. At first I wasn't sure what they expected from me, other than the usual: to smile and be the supportive rock-n-roll wife. It wasn't until I was on the set—my home—that I discovered I was supposed to be distinctly terse and demanding toward Ted; i.e., a bitch. Certainly no one in their right mind can rule over the true alpha male (Ted); still, I wasn't thrilled about making my television debut as a Susan Lucci–type shrew for the whole world to see. Especially since I'm usually the one who walks out on arguments and desperately tries to calmly talk things through during heated debates with my husband. Although I made my intentions clear to the producers, everything changed dramatically when Ted was resistant to be pushed into the Motor City Madman character VH1 was expecting.

An army of black-Ninja-clad videographers equipped with an arsenal of cameras and cables swarmed onto our home and covered it like spiders spinning webs. Within hours my garage had been transformed into a makeshift television studio. A wall of monitors, amps, and other digital recording devices was set up over my Suburban tire tracks. Our precious hounds certainly must have wondered what on earth was going on as nearly fifty people and dozens of vehicles came in and out of our house, drove up and down the driveway, and basically assaulted our once pristine compound for ninety-six hours.

Parts of my home were reorganized and redecorated without my knowledge. Some of that was okay, and some just took me by surprise. One overly cheery gentleman I hadn't seen before bounded into our house and announced, "Hi! I have your new door."

"My new door?" I asked, confused. I didn't remember ordering a new door.

"Yeah, for your laundry room, just off the kitchen," he said as he scanned the house and homed in on the target. "Right here." And he went to work installing my *new door.*

I noticed that this door had a one-way mirror cut through the center of it and quickly sought out one of the producers to see why my house was being blessed with this new decoration. It's true, people act differently when a camera is hovering over them, and now with this one-way mirror, more of our new videographer friends could see us (me) in the kitchen—but we couldn't see them. There was also some sort of robocam installed in the corner of my dining room that could zoom in on my nose hair while I was washing dishes twenty feet away in the kitchen. The robocam was entirely operated by more of our new gentlemen friends in my garage. I had to be careful about stuffing down that last bite of cake. Two or three people were constantly following Ted with video cameras and a boom microphone just in case he said anything wild or crazy. And we were supposed to carry on as if everything were normal.

The contestants' goal, of course, was to survive doing chores with Ted, but not just any chores. The contests included manure hauling, deer skinning (which wasn't much fun for the vegetarian girl), karaoke, and even paintball. What was supposed to make the whole show entertaining was for the contestants to fear Ted's wrath, but there was a slight problem. Ted just couldn't manufacture unwarranted anger. These people were actually nice, and it's difficult to suddenly begin to scream at folks after you've just offered them a cup of coffee. And they were asking Ted to be their idea of *Ted,* not for him to portray a fictional character, and that's what he was sticking to. He can only be ruthless and overbearing if the situation warrants it.

The funny thing is that on any given day at the Nugent Ranch ten things go wrong, and you can hear my husband yelling from here to Boise. He has a short temper, but a quick wit. We never know when so many things go wrong whether he'll wind up telling silly stories and making us laugh, or getting more angry—which, of course, is not much fun. Hence, *Surviving Nugent.*

The problem we were having with this shoot was that everything seemed to be going well. The contestants were getting along and doing the chores just fine. In the eyes of the VH1 staff, Ted suddenly became the *Motor City Nice Guy.* After the first contest, the producers came to me and asked if there was any way I could talk to my husband and get him to act angrier. "Sure," I said. "I'll tell him to pretend that I crashed the Bronco or I took the family on a shopping orgy at Neiman Marcus and spent a bunch of money . . . something like that. Then he can imagine he's yelling at me. Maybe that will make him feel more comfortable."

When that didn't work, the producers said that there would be no show and clearly seemed frustrated with Ted's congenial behavior toward his guests. So I had an intervention with Ted, along with his assistant, Linda Peterson, and his manager, Doug Banker. We tried to explain the dire situation we were in. The pilot was based on Ted's Motor City Madman image—an image that had come from thirty-five years of screaming at concerts, fighting for the Second Amendment, sporting a ponytail when he's fifty-four years old, and every other rebellious thing we could think of. He wasn't buying it. He said he felt unnatural being mean to strangers and added, "No can do."

Although the show was only a pilot, a lot of people were working very hard on the project, and I feared that at any moment Ted would just pull the plug and send everyone home. It had taken months of planning just to put this pilot together—not to mention more money than most people make in a year. I knew that given the chance, Ted was exactly the guy the producers had in mind. He was every bit as raw and as wild and as intense as they imagined.

After they shot the manure scene, the contestants came back into our basement and tracked dirt and, yes, manure, into our house. One of the producers came upstairs and asked me for a mop and some cleaning supplies.

I was battling a low-grade headache from the onslaught of people traipsing in and out, in and out, and in and out of my house, and then I remembered the custom zebra-striped carpeting in our lower level. Suddenly I took on the rage that Ted was apparently lacking.

"They tracked manure in my basement?"

The producer nodded.

"Okay, now I'm pissed."

"Good," he said with a glimmer of hope in his eyes. "Let's go with it."

And while he instructed the camera operator to be ready to roll tape in the basement, I grabbed some cleaning supplies.

I realized the show desperately needed something intriguing. Maybe if Mrs. Nugent really did go ballistic, things might get juicy, even if that was exactly the way I didn't want to be seen.

"How much do you want me to milk this?" I asked.

They said something like *a lot* or *as much as you can,* so I went downstairs and milked it for all I had. I saw mud on the floor and yelled, "Okay, you guys are guests here at our home, and you're tracking in all this mud and you're not even cleaning it up!" Then I started throwing the cleaning supplies at them and ordered, "Here, clean it up!" I really went wild, but I got my carpet cleaned in the process. Certainly I wouldn't get an Academy Award, but a lot was riding on my husband's shoulders and for some reason he just needed a little help. Maybe, I prayed, the next day would be better.

The second day of shooting got better or worse, depending upon how you look at it, because things finally started to go wrong for VH1, just like they do for us. The contestants were shocked—as I was—to discover that they had to spend the night in our horse barn in the middle of winter with no heat, and it was cold and snowing outside. It started looking like a real *Survivor*-type show. They were complaining and whimpering, and Ted was getting cranky, too. Ah! Maybe we were getting somewhere. There were even people spending the night in our garage to monitor the television cameras through the night. I remembered the robocam in the kitchen just before I was about to make Ted a late-night snack.

"Sorry, honey, but I'm not going into the kitchen in my nightie just to make you popcorn," I announced. I could tell that the chaos was finally getting to him. That and the fact that he'd have to go to bed without his favorite homemade popcorn made him even more irritated, which was good in this case.

Ted was scheduled to wake the contestants at the crack of dawn by blasting "The Star-Spangled Banner" over speakers that had already been hidden in the horse barn hay. Unfortunately, when Ted plugged in and started playing, the speakers just hummed at first. Ted was quickly becoming an Angry Young Man. After a few moments a technician fixed the speakers, but Ted was clearly irritated. I don't know what it is, but things always seem to go wrong in Ted's World.

The next activity was paintballing, and only Ted was to be riding a horse. All the contestants had on protective gear and were supposed to try to make it out to some bales of hay in a field—the bales sported flags that had hundred-dollar bills taped to them—all while avoiding getting hit by Ted's rapid-fire paintball. My husband hadn't been riding for a while and he is fifty-four years old, so naturally I was slightly worried about him being physically able to endure it. It took about four hours for the VH1 producers and crew to set up for the shoot, and by that time Ted was exactly the man they'd come to see. It had started snowing and it was cold. He'd been sitting on the horse for most of those four hours and his legs were sore. Of course he'd also been making witty, cocky, mostly outrageous comments all day that literally had the crew rolling with laughter. *He was back in the saddle again.*

Ted rode the horse as if he were twenty, but I was still nervous. I suppose that's my job, as a rock star's wife—as any wife. No matter where Ted is—on stage, doing a radio or television interview, or riding a horse around for hours in the middle of winter—I worry that he'll be safe, healthy, and happy. I suppose that's the main focus of being married to a rock-n-roll musician. Just like the wife of a doctor, or a lawyer, or a teacher, or a pilot, I worry about my husband. But Ted was galloping and running that horse one-handed like a professional cowboy, turning on a dime, hunting down the contestants with the paintball gun one by one as they scattered, ran, and tried to hide from *the Nuge.* It was almost as if Ted had been born for this game, and he had been practicing for months. It certainly looked like he was having fun. I even caught the producers smiling.

Later that night, when the filming was over and the show was wrapped, one of the contestants was in our barn crying. The camera operators were winding up their cords and unraveling the webs they'd spun and everyone was busy picking up their belongings, but this one young lady just broke down sobbing. Ted told me later that he'd approached her and discovered why she was crying: The snow reminded her of her home. This pretty young girl sat with my husband

and told him how sad she was because she'd suddenly remembered that the holidays were only weeks away and she couldn't spend Christmas with her family.

It was the Motor City Madman, my wild, crazy, uninhibited, irreverent husband, who comforted this girl when she needed a shoulder to cry on, hugging and consoling her. He told her about our friends Zac Martin and Chip Stewart who, through no fault of their own, had received real blows from life-threatening illnesses but never, ever let it get to them. He reminded this woman that she was very healthy and able to walk and run and dance and sing. He told her that life was really about the quality connections we have with people and that those relationships with her family members would always be there when they were ready and when she was. She thanked him, and then Ted gave her and everyone else little gifts for coming and sharing some time with us at our home.

I learned some valuable lessons that weekend. I realized that I'd truly enjoyed meeting all those visitors I might otherwise have never had a chance to meet. And that each time we meet someone new, we take a little piece of them with us in our hearts, and they take a piece of us. Eventually, our hearts can be full.

I recognized that it might sometimes rain or snow when we least expect it. Life doesn't always work out the way we want it to, hope it does, or dream that it will when we're young and naive. We need to be prepared for the worst. Bring an umbrella just in case it rains, and if it doesn't, we'll be pleasantly surprised. If it pours cats and dogs for forty days and forty nights, we'll just have to go to plan B. There is a plan B, right?

Watching my husband through years of being kicked down by swindling managers, business partners, and even employees, who combined have taken more money than most people make in a lifetime, helped me see where he gets his strength. Like the Energizer Bunny, Ted just keeps going and going. He rarely stops to dwell on how many times we've been ripped off and cheated. He'd rather look at the goodness in humanity: the friendly faces at the coffee shop, his old hunting buddies, his family, his friends, and of course all of his faithful hounds. There certainly are many things in life that we could be depressed about, but I can honestly say I've never seen my husband sad in fourteen years, and it's not as if we haven't had rough times to deal with. His foundation is solid. Like the most indestructible building, he doesn't sway. He knows he's made mistakes but he learns, upgrades, and keeps on going.

I realize that my husband isn't the man I married. He's more than the guy I met at the radio station fourteen years ago. He's more than wickedly funny or stunningly charming. He's more than just a guy who gets up on stage and plays guitar. He is an intensely caring and compassionate man who is every bit as imperfect as I am. I learned that I married the right guy.

While America just can't seem to get enough of its reality-based television, I feel it's high time that someone actually come out and discuss what goes on after the cameras stop rolling. What happens when everyone goes home? While networks are scrambling for more and more *Survivor*-based shows, no one seems to care what happens to the people who are left behind—the losers, or the non-winners. Being married to a celebrity is often like a consolation prize. At times, during introductions, people shake my hand while they're hopelessly stargazing at Ted.

What I've written here in this book wasn't easy—but it was real, and sometimes it's the authentic moments we share in our lives that bring us closer. It makes us tougher too. My darkest nights challenged me to become a better person by sharing this story and peeling back a painful layer of thin onion skin. I am not the same timid person I was before the animal rights activists attacked me or before the struggles Ted and I endured. I've changed. As wine gets better with age, so too do we, and I've recognized my weaknesses and worked on them.

Premarital relationships are often regrettable. Someone is eventually left behind, or worse, pregnant and unmarried. Ted and I were lucky that we ended up in love and married for the long term.

Always enthralled by learning, even amidst the chaos of worldwide travels, managing ten businesses, and raising a family, I acquired a master's degree in metaphysics, reminding myself daily, if not hourly, that I could do more, I could do better. And with knowledge, I believe, comes power. Groupies, swindlers, and hustlers are everywhere, in every type of business, and I now prefer not to give them my power. I'm learning. From the time I met and married my husband, my confidence levels have soared, not to the highest mountain—yet, but I'm continually striving for upgrade in myself and in my surroundings. We all make mistakes and we must all get up the next day and try again. Sharing generous doses of encouragement and love with family, friends, and everyone I meet is what I truly strive to do. Giving, now, is what feeds my soul. Each day, every day we must continue to pursue our greatest dreams and make our own mark on the world. Who knows what spectacular dreams are ahead for the Nugent Tribe? Will Ted Nugent really run for governor of Michigan in 2006?

Damned If Ya Do

Ted Nugent, "Craveman"—2002
Lyrics by Ted Nugent

I don't care if you respect me.
I'm branded like a dog.
I expect you to reject me.
I'm sure it won't take long.
Look at me on the frontlines,
I ain't afraid of no shit.
I must be outta my mind,
can't git enuf of it.
I don't care if you think I'm a loser,
I don't care if you think I am God!
I don't know if I will win or lose her,
I just know I'm cryin out loud.
And I'm Damned if I do,
Damned if I don't.

References

Ban Breathnach, Sarah. *Something More.* New York: Warner Books, 1998.

Centers for Disease Control. "National and State-Specific Pregnancy Rates Among Adolescents." Atlanta: CDC, 1997.

"Tracking the Hidden Epidemics: Trends in STDs in the U.S." Atlanta: CDC, 2000.

Cooney, Teresa. "Broken Hearts: Kids Suffer Long-Term Harm When Parents Slip into Adultery," *Denver Rocky Mountain News,* 1998.

Duncan, Homer. "Humanistic Sex Education in the Public Schools." Lubbock, TX: World-Wide Missionary Crusader, Inc. 1980.

Gallagher, Maggie. "Fatherless Boys Grow Up into Dangerous Men." *Wall Street Journal,* December 1, 1998.

Larson, Joan Mathews, Ph.D. *7 Weeks to Emotional Healing.* New York: Random House, 1999.

Mitchell, William, Jr. *Adultery: Facing Its Reality.* New York: Mitchell Reports Professional Investigations, 2002.

Pollack, William, Ph.D. *Real Boys: Rescuing Our Sons from the Myths of Boyhood.* New York: Henry Holt and Company, 2002.

Rockefeller Commission, The. *The Rockefeller Commission on Population Growth and the American Future,* www.population-security.org/rockefeller, Washington D.C.: 2002.

Roush, Matt. "Reflecting Values." *USA Today,* 1996.

Samuals, Dr. Dave. *Know Hunting.* Cheat Lake, WV: Know Hunting Publications, 2002.

Schuman, Dr. Helen, and Dr. William Thetford. *A Course in Miracles*. Glen Allen, CA: The Foundation for Inner Peace, 1992.

"Stop Eco-Violence!" *News Alerts*. Wilsonville, OR: 2002

Vanzant, Iyanla. *Until Today*. New York: Simon & Schuster, 2000.

Weil, Bonnie Eaker, and Ruth Winter. *Adultery: The Forgivable Sin*. Fern Park, FL: Hastings House Publications, 1994.

Weiss, Mark. "Eco-Terrorists Frustrate FBI." *San Francisco Chronicle*, February 3, 2002.

INDEX

Note: Page numbers in boldface indicate photographs.

C

D

E

F

G